RUSSELL MOCKRIDGE
The Man In Front

RUSSELL MOCKRIDGE
The Man In Front

MARTIN CURTIS

M

MELBOURNE BOOKS

Published by Melbourne Books
Level 9, 100 Collins Street,
Melbourne, VIC, 3000
Australia
www.melbournebooks.com.au
info@melbournebooks.com.au

The author and publisher gratefully
acknowledge the Mockridge family for
permission to use extracts from *My World
On Wheels* by Russell Mockridge
© copyright Mockridge family, and for the
use of family photographs.

National Library of Australia Cataloguing-in-
Publication entry
Author: Curtis, Martin.
Title: Russell Mockridge : The Man In Front
ISBN: 9781877096549 (pbk.)
Subjects: Mockridge, Russell 1928-1958.
Cyclists–Australia–Biography.
Dewey Number: 796.6092

Front cover photo:
Russell Mockridge at the finish of the
Warrnambool to Melbourne Road Race, 1956,
at the Melbourne Showground.
Photo: The *Herald and Weekly Times* photographic
collection

Back cover photo:
Russell Mockridge riding in the Ronde
de Monaco, 1955
Photo: *Miroir Sprint*

Book design: Ning Xue
Printed in Australia by Trojan Press

This book is dedicated to the valiant riders of the 20th century, who paved the way for their successors in the 21st century.

Life is mainly froth and bubble
Two things stand like stone
Kindness in another's struggle
Courage in your own

Adam Lindsay Gordon

Acknowledgements

The author thanks Lindy Mockridge, Elinor Brown, Russell Smith, Jim Taylor, John Tressider, John Beasley, Lionel Cox, Graham Huddlestone, Josh Huddlestone, John Trevorrow, Trevor Wykes, Russell Holmesby, Paul Amy, Steve Duffy, Colin Moyle, Ted Hopkins, Col Davies, Gary Tippet, Neil Wilson, Bill Vary, Laura Jeanne Gobal, Phillip Curtis and Lyn Curtis for their support and encouragement during the research and development of this project. Special thanks go to publisher David Tenenbaum, who instantly recognised the significance of the Mockridge story.

Mockridge the Cycling Legend

They say he was phenomenal, a legend in his time,
A wizard on the track or road, but cut down in his prime
Born in Nineteen Twenty Eight, and at cycling rose to fame,
He carved a place in history, Russell Mockridge is his name.

When they speak of cycling legends, Opperman, Patterson and such,
Don't forget the mighty Mockridge, for he gave the game so much
Geelong was where he spent his youth, when cycling was at its height,
He came one day to try his luck, on his worn out roadster bike.

Thick glasses and sandshoes, he just didn't look the part,
So the officials, feeling sorry, gave the lad a decent start
"Do you mind if I just stay in front", he said with a quiet grin,
Then away he pedalled furiously, and that was his first win.

Next week they gave him not so much, but he beat them just the same,
He then recorded fastest time, and from there went on to fame
A relentless racing dynamo, wrote the critics of that era,
Who could burn the opposition off, without worry or of fear.

Many were the races that he won all "round the world"
With many leading riders toppled, so the legend was unfurled
Les McLean, Jack Hoobin and Mac Sloane to name a few,
Were just some of the riders to see his back wheel too.

In the Commonwealth and Olympic Games he also had a win,
In Nineteen Fifty and Fifty Two, there was no stopping him
Even in the tandem race where he teamed with Lionel Cox,
There was no one who could touch him, he was super, he was tops

So life rolled on for Russell, as he followed the racing game,
In Australia and in Europe, everybody new his name,
With iron legs and giant heart, a gentleman of sorts,
Loved by those who knew him, and a credit to the sport

T'was a sad day in September, in Nineteen Fifty Eight,
On his last race in Australia, Russell Mockridge met his fate,
It was on the Tour of Gippsland, when the race had just begun,
He collided with a city bus, and his race with life was done

And so a life is ended, and a legend it is born,
A Nation weeps in sorrow and a woman's heart is torn
But you left behind a memory, of that you can be proud,
No, we'll not forget you Russell, and we sing your praises loud

Brian A Gale
Margaret River, Western Australia

Contents

Introduction

RUSSELL MOCKRIDGE WAS arguably the best all-round Australian cyclist of the post-World War II era.

Mockridge won gold medals as a sprinter, set world and Olympic records in the velodrome, and then slogged it out in road races where only true grit and inner strength would get you across the line. Mostly he was first across the line.

He left a significant legacy. Thanks partly to Mockridge the dividing line between amateur and professional cyclist has been removed. Mockridge's battle with Olympic officials in the lead up to the Helsinki Olympic Games in the 1950s exposed the stupidity of the demarcation.

Mockridge grew up in Geelong and used to race his brother to Torquay in the summer holidays just for the pure fun of it. Mockridge loved the life of a cyclist, the pure joy of taking in the sights and sounds and riding faster than anyone else. He never lost that love. For the record Mockridge and his brother used to ride the 23kms between Geelong and Torquay, on heavy old bikes, with their lunches in canvas bags on their back, in 30 minutes.

Geelong is rich in cycling lore. Cadel Evans lives at Barwon Heads. Mockridge's mentor was Hubert Opperman, who rode the Tour de France in the 1930s and then became the federal member of parliament for Corio. It was a list of Opperman records that got Mockridge interested in racing. He paced himself against Opperman's times on weekend rides in the countryside around Geelong and found he was competitive.

Though he rode as a *domestique* for an international team in the 1955 Tour de France, he was no-body's servant. Back in Australia, his races against Sid Patterson and international stars at the Olympic velodrome in Melbourne and at the West velodrome in Geelong are legend.

Contemporary cyclists have much to gain from a knowledge of Russell Mockridge's life. It was a life dedicated to health and fitness, the sport of cycling, high ideals and family. Even in death he left a lesson. Mockridge was killed in a collision with a bus only minutes into a professional road race. We can never assume we are safe on the roads.

John Trevorrow, 2008

John Trevorrow, originally from Morwell, won the Sun Tour three times, in 1975, 1977 and 1979. He retired from racing in 1981 after national and international success and now runs a cycle shop and cycle event management business in Geelong.

Prologue

By 1949 Russell Mockridge was the next big thing in Australian cycling. He had come from obscurity to the 1948 Olympic Games in two years, and commentators were loud in their predictions about the 21-year-old's potential.

From the Australian Cyclist, June 1949
By Stan Mullany

IN MY LONG experience in Australian cycling I have seen sensational rises to fame – I saw Jack Fitzgerald win at his first try, and then go on to world fame – I saw Bob Spears, Dunc Gray and Hubert Opperman confound critics preparatory to winning honours in other lands – and I saw other wheelmen win their way to fame by sheer persistency. As I walk the path of memory musing over the exploits of these and other Australians of the great past, I am completely baffled in my efforts to find one rider who can compare in detail with Geelong's Russell Mockridge.

To have risen from total obscurity to Olympic status as a road force within one year, is an achievement hitherto unknown in the annals of Australian amateur cycling.

It is common knowledge now how this manly young sporting enthusiast, after excelling at most other sports, wandered along to the start of a bicycle race and asked could he ride in it.

Ill-equipped with heavy machine, with street shoes, and minus the aid of all other accessories that make for speed, young Mockridge caused a major sensation by gaining first and fastest honours in that initial attempt as a bike rider, an effort that was destined to place him on the path to world fame as a road rider.

Since that memorable entry into cycle racing, Mockridge has gone on to all manner of State and National successes, and this, plus his superb sportsmanship makes him one of the most valuable assets ever possessed by Australian amateur cycling.

This rider's worth as a propaganda medium is enhanced by an attainment rarely achieved by the average athlete – he is capable of holding any audience as an after-dinner speaker.

With road honours thick upon him, Russell Mockridge, an unknown quantity as a track rider, decides to 'have a ride or two' at North Essendon Board Track, merely as a pipe-opener for the road season.

Chatting with him as the riders sat on their machines, awaiting the starting gong in his first track race, I was surprised to hear his father give this last minute advice; "If that leg can't stand up to the strain, don't persevere, Russell – just pull off."

I then found out that, just as Mockridge entered road racing under difficulties, he was to receive his track baptism under the crushing handicap of leg ligament and ankle trouble, for which he was under the care of masseur Ernie Saunders.

In that initial handicap final, Mockridge, after finishing a close second, was quizzed by me thus: "What gear did you push?" His retort was: "I was geared at 96." His father, who was present at this interview, confirmed Russell's statement.

Apparently my query on his gearage had led to closer scrutiny, for some little time after, Mr Mockridge sr came up to me on the arena and said: "Your surmise was right on the mark – do you know a check up has revealed that a '14' instead of a '13' back sprocket was inadvertently affixed to Russell's machine, making the gear ratio 86 instead of the essential 96?"

The real merit of this initial track performance lies in this fact – Mockridge, with a leg injury and pushing a 'Cotton Reel' gear while riding high on the track all the way, had outridden all but one outmarker in a field of seasoned track riders.

At his second outing as a track rider, he won the handicap from virtual scratch and, in the subsequent scratch race he came from a seemingly impossible position to snatch a brilliant victory, thus completing a double success, an achievement hitherto performed only by Olympian Sid Patterson.

They are the inside facts of Mockridge's entry into the ranks of track riders.

With full knowledge of Mockridge's capabilities as a class road rider, I am going to say right now that concentration along the right lines would eventually lead him to world class as a track exponent.

Mockridge is not a glamour rider in that he is not a stylist in the saddle, lacking the poise of a Sid Patterson, a Bill Guyatt, or a Jack Walsh.

But his speed-making qualities are most deceptive in that his powers of momentum are hidden in his seemingly effortless gait that likens him in this regard to the mighty Bob Spears.

He has this in common with Spears – he is right behind those handlebars in such a decisive manner that affords the maximum benefit from his strong and uncanny pedalling ability.

In simple language, his whole force is behind the handlebars, a lost art in modern track racing techniques.

The average track rider flies that last lap with arms bent outwards in the style of a jockey, with little or no driving power behind those handlebars.

Mockridge is not a copybook rider, but his unorthodox

methods in most things now give rise to the suggestion that copybook methods are due for revision.

To me, Russell Mockridge is the modern wheel enigma in that, with his known possibilities as a road champion, I am certain he would develop world class as a track rider, under the direct supervision of a Jack Fitzgerald, a Tom Carey, or a Boggerty Horton.

Stan Mullany, *Australian Cyclist*, June 1949

Chapter 1

Starting from Scratch

Once there was a way to get back homeward
Once there was a way to get back home
Sleep pretty darling do not cry
And I will sing a lullabye

"Golden Slumbers", *Abbey Road*, The Beatles

THE STORY BEGINS with a second-hand bike. It was a bike with a pedigree – the father's bike, which, as the eldest son, the boy hoped to inherit. The death of its original owner, the great cyclist Russell Mockridge, had left a great sadness. The bike was revered by father and son. In provincial post-war Australia, it carried with it the power of possibility.

In the towns and suburbs of 1950s Australia, in the humble fibro-cement homes where the baby boom echoed loudly, success with a bicycle was a road out of an ordinary life, a route to another place. In Australian country towns the local heroes raced around gravel tracks circling the footy ground. In Melbourne, part of the legacy of the 1956 Olympics was an outdoor stadium with timber decking laid top to bottom, where the roar of the riders as they hurled around the steep circuit made for a powerful, edgy, soundtrack.

This was a blue-collar world. There were no stockbrokers or financial planners riding bikes in the 1950s. The world of cycling was a bit like the world of boxing, where a strong competitor could make money and a reputation on the back of his strength and talent, and where the possibilities of escape from the certainties of school and work opened up like a dream world of undiscovered, verdant valleys. This was a boy's world of heroes and supermen, and I was connected to this dream through Russell Mockridge's Healing racing bike.

Mockridge's world on wheels came crashing down on Saturday morning, September 13, 1958, minutes into the annual Tour of Gippsland road race, when a bus drove into the path of the five-man scratch bunch as they rode through the intersection of Clayton and Dandenong roads.

Thirty-year-old Mockridge and his mate Jim Taylor hit the bus. Mockridge slid under and seconds later was dead, his head crushed by the rear wheels of the Oakleigh to Box Hill bus. To add insult to injury, after the bus stopped, it rolled back and crushed the legs that had won gold medals for Australia six years earlier. The news spread quickly. Mockridge's rival, Sid Patterson, quit the race out of respect. Mockridge's father, Bob, was called to the secretary's office at Flemington racetrack and told that his dual Olympic gold medallist son was dead under a bus.

Mockridge's wife, Irene, who was following the riders in a car, witnessed the collision. Her dreams of a happy future with her husband and young child were crushed that sunny spring morning just as emphatically as her husband's head and body. Crushed also were a nation of supporters who had followed Mockridge's sporting achievements, his battles with officials and his curious, understated, public style.

For a seven-year-old Catholic boy enduring a "Sisters without Mercy" upbringing, where the nightly family rosary was that week dedicated to Russell's non-Catholic eternal soul, his death brought noticeable sadness to the parents who were putting their lives back together after the upheavals of World War II.

The bike that had belonged to Russell Mockridge fitted into this narrative. People died in the war. Mockridge died on the road. Life was all about "getting on with it." Kids at school had medals from family members killed in the war. We had the bike that had belonged to Russell Mockridge and I loaded it up with magic powers.

Mockridge was the gifted but troubled rider from Geelong whose death at an unremarkable southeast Melbourne intersection robbed the nation of a great sportsman and human being.

In 1999, I met Mockridge's widow, Irene, his partner and confidante, with whom he had been making life plans, including a return to Europe and another crack at the Tour de France.

I felt, after first meeting Irene, that she was still grieving. She launched a vitriolic attack on the sport and the officials who ran it.

She asked me, "What were grown men with families doing taking those sorts of risks and hardly making any money out of it?"

I later came to believe that while the memories were painful, Irene had recovered from the catastrophe that was her husband's death. Like the war widows, she had done as requested and "got on with it." She had stopped being Russell Mockridge's widow and she was irritated that people wanted to drag her back to that bleak place. One life ended there but she rebuilt her life, and built her daughter's life, yet no one was interested in that story.

Nothing can bring Russell Mockridge back, but a new generation of cyclists might learn something from his style, values and high ideals. Professional cycling was never for the faint-hearted: doping scandals, race fixing, dodgy promoters and circus-style promotions were par for the course.

Mockridge set high standards in his personal and professional lives and gained public respect, if not the praise of fellow cyclists, for doing so.

These days the road system is more contested and congested than ever. Cyclists, high- and low-profile, continue to die pursuing their sport or simply travelling to and from work. Animosity between riders and motorists seems to be at an all-time high. Every year around 40 cyclists die on Australian roads, almost without exception in collisions with motor vehicles.

In Victoria the death toll averages around a dozen a year, a downward trend at a time when bike sales are going up.

In 1924, Don Kirkham, a dairy farmer from Carrum, Melbourne, was knocked down by a drunk driver on Point Nepean Road. Kirkham was the first Australian to ride the Tour de France. He later died from the injuries he sustained.

In 1982, a 63-year-old out for a fitness ride was hit by a milk tanker near his home in Maffra, Victoria. He was Keith Rowley, the winner of the inaugural 1952 *Sun* Tour.

In 1984, the energetic Nino Borsari, an Italian star who came to Melbourne to race the local heroes and decided to stay and open a business in Carlton, was struck from behind by a hit-and-run driver and sustained head injuries.

In 2005, the hopes of women's cycling in Australia were dashed when a young German motorist, apparently swerving to avoid a bird, ploughed into Amy Gillett, who was killed, and three of her team-mates, who were seriously injured, on a training ride on a provincial German road.

Ironically, Amy Gillett's maiden name was Safe. Forty-seven years after Russell Mockridge's death under a bus, Amy's death at the hands of a distracted motorist reminds us that the roads are anything but safe and that cyclists can pay a high price for pursuing their sport or hobby.

Then there's the roll-call of un-famous cyclists who've died, like Trent Jones, aged 29, who died after he was knocked off his bike and thrown into the path of a truck travelling along Mate Street, Albury, on Thursday, July 19, 2007.

Jones was a rehabilitation nurse at Albury Base Hospital and was on his way home from work. I only learnt about his death through an obituary in my old school newsletter. His was another senseless death; another life laid to waste.

Australian cyclist Cadel Evans, runner-up in the 2007 and 2008 Tour de France, told *The Age* in January 2008 that there was nowhere on earth where he felt less safe on his bike than in Australia.

Chapter 2

Love and Theft

MY **WORLD ON** wheels came crashing down when the Mockridge bike, by now repainted and re-chromed, was stolen from the rear of a block of flats in Prahran in 1978.

I was working an early shift doing police rounds for the afternoon Melbourne *Herald* and knocking off around 1pm.

Melbourne's gift to cycling, the beach road that hugs Port Phillip Bay from St Kilda to Frankston, had captured me. It was a glorious way to spend an autumn afternoon and great to be riding again after a spell that roughly coincided with the rock 'n' roll years of 15 to 25.

I remember my dominant emotion over the theft was anger: at myself for not having the bike locked, and at anyone who looked in the slightest way suspicious. In welfare-dependent, drug-using Prahran in the late 1970s, I had cast a wide net.

I convinced myself that a local bike shop was doing a trade in stolen bike parts and I obsessed about likely suspects in the block of flats where my partner, Lyn, and I lived in Peel Street.

But this didn't bring it back, nor did the police who had rape and murder cases to investigate. Bicycle theft ranked below shoplifting. It was a nuisance. No one was ever arrested.

But I remained intrigued by this tenuous link to the

Mockridge story. It was a father–son connection, a memory of my dad in his rough-hewn shed, repairing, Depression-style with fencing wire or a second-hand nut and bolt, something that should have been thrown out long ago. The Mockridge bike didn't get this rough handling. It was a marvel of engineering and revered as such.

When I started researching Mockridge's life and met Irene, I realised how trivial and self-obsessed this other story was. I had lost a piece of machinery. Irene had lost her life partner; her daughter Lindy would grow up without a dad.

But a powerful memory stuck with me. No bike I consequently owned seemed to match it. I mourned the Simplex gears and the Brooks saddle. Most of all, I missed the idea of pedigree, or heritage. It was a talisman, an object of power and significance, a charm.

I could get the facts of Mockridge's life from many sources, including his own posthumously published autobiography, *My World On Wheels,* but the journalist in me wanted more. I wanted to know him better. His book speaks about the state of the sport in the 1950s and there is a good, first-person description of his solo 1955 Tour de France, but in the style of the time, there are few personal insights.

The person who could unlock the door to Russell Mockridge's life would not be a willing player in my quest. I initially thought Irene's curtness was a defence to cover her grief and loss. She was justifiably angry that the intersection where Mockridge died was not patrolled by police or cycling officials that morning.

In a moment the cycling world lost one of its champions but she lost her future. She was angry about the outcome of the inquest, which called the death an accident, and she suggested justice had not been served. Both Irene and Mockridge's father claimed the organisers of the race had escaped proper investigation and that the intersection should have been patrolled.

The fact that five of the finest cyclists in the country, the men held back by the handicap system for an hour to give the lesser riders a chance, were not protected, or monitored, except by Irene Mockridge driving an Austin A40, is, by current standards, negligent.

But it was a mistake to see Irene Mockridge only as the long-grieving, victim–widow. Her frustration with journalists and the cycling world was that we saw her only as Russell Mockridge's widow. We saw her in a time capsule that, if it could be opened, would reveal the insights into this very private man that we needed in order to write the next chapter.

Mockridge was a man of few words. His aloofness was widely read as snobbishness. He'd been to Geelong College and he'd worked as a journalist for the *Geelong Advertiser*. He was a friend of Percy Cerutty, the eccentric athletics coach who preached an alternate lifestyle modelled on a home-grown understanding of the lives of the Spartans and Greek philosophy.

Mockridge was an educated, literate, questioning man living in an unquestioning era.

Australia was in the big sleep of the Menzies era. He was unsure of what he wanted to do with his life. He tried journalism, he flirted with the idea of theological studies. But he was drawn back to cycling because he was so damn good at it, despite the handicaps of short-sightedness and shyness, which left him isolated among the pack of happy-go-lucky blokes who shared his destiny. He was an outsider. He turned professional a year after the 1952 Helsinki Olympics, eliminating himself from the next Olympics, the hometown Melbourne event of 1956.

The painfully shy Mockridge was a seeker of truth. He described himself as a confused and emotionally unstable 20-year-old who sought enlightenment through the Anglican priesthood. He sought a moral context for his life. He wanted to live an honest and honourable life in a rough-and-tumble, carnival world of promoters, pesky journalists and thrill-seeking crowds. He refused to accept the Olympic fidelity bond, which committed the athletes of 1952 to remain amateur for two years after the Helsinki Olympics because he had plans to turn professional and explore the big-time European road and race circuit.

He could not, in good conscience, sign the bond. After a lot of hand-wringing and brow-beating played out on the national political and media stage, he agreed to a one-year bond.

He was the odd man out in an underworld of fixing and dealing. His stance attracted the attention of the wider community.

And he loved Irene Pritchard, who he met on the *Otranto* in 1952, on the voyage to Europe and the Olympics. Irene was a smart working-class girl from Richmond with the travel bug. Their later three years together in Europe would be happy times. They were Australians enjoying being out of their comfort zone and "on the Continent."

The parochial, black-and-white world of 1950s Australia, the "Little Lord Fauntleroy" jibes, were in their place – in the Antipodes. He was deeply in love with Irene and, after 1954, with fatherhood.

And he rode *la Grande Boucle*, the big lap of France. In 1955 he became the first Australian to complete the Tour de France in 24 years – since Hubert Opperman in 1931. He was in the Luxembourg-International team, but the English-speaking oddity was excluded from the team strategy in the early part of the race. Towards the end of the three weeks he became valuable to Charly Gaul, the captain and star of the Luxembourg team, who eventually took third place in the classic.

Mockridge was placed 64th out of the 69 who finished. He'd helped Gaul win, but the financial rewards were not to be shared. He was an amateur when it came to avarice.

Just before he was killed in September 1958, he had made plans with Irene to cut short the Victorian summer track season of 1958–59 so he could be in Europe in January to start training for the Italian and French road season of 1959. In Australia he was unbeatable on road or track. There were great expectations. Properly supported, he was a Tour de France stage winner because of his stamina and sprinting power. He could make money in Europe, where professional cycling was lucrative and popularly supported. He'd learnt a lot from his first tour of Europe. He was going to have another crack at the big time.

This is a good story, I tell myself as I puff up some minor hill on a veterans' ride.

The coroner found his death was accidental, but the family believed justice had not been done.

Cycling officialdom had escaped any criticism by coroner J. M. Duggan, who performed the ritual inquest two months after the collision.

The "inquisition" held upon the body of Edward Russell Mockridge, by James Michael Duggan, "gentleman and

Coroner of our Lady the Queen", found that on the 13th day of September 1958, at the intersection of Princes Highway and Clayton Road, Mockridge died from "injuries then and there accidentally received when the bicycle he was riding in an easterly direction along Princes Highway, Clayton, whilst participating as a competitor in a cycling event, came into collision with a motor vehicle which was proceeding in a northerly direction in Clayton road and he then fell to the ground and was run over by the said vehicle."

Mockridge's father Bob used plainer English when he explained the circumstances of the collision to me in 1998.

"The bus came from their right. The intersection was supposed to be monitored by cycling officials. Several hit the side of the bus. Russell went under and the back wheels rolled over his head. The driver got out but forgot to put the brakes on and the bus rolled over him again."

Russell's head, his father said, under several tonnes of Reo bus, "popped like a watermelon."

Irene, driving the family car with three-year-old Lindy, was minutes behind and arrived to see the bloody reality of her husband's death.

Another wife thrown into the maelstrom was Thelma Young, the wife of John Young. The two cyclists prostrate on the road were wearing the blue Victorian jersey, the same one her husband was wearing that day. She was spared. John Young, with more time to react, braked and swerved and clipped the end of the bus, but stayed upright.

I pursued Irene in the hope of learning more about her husband in order to write his story. She was difficult and uncooperative. By 1998, on the 40th anniversary of her husband's death, she'd moved on.

Irene had been devastated and gutted by the loss of her husband, but she had created a new life for herself and her daughter that had nothing to do with cycling.

Did I have the right to persist in the face of disinterest and opposition? What were the boundaries around my pursuit of her husband's story?

I would think about these questions on bike rides. I remained fascinated with the Mockridge story. I found cycling officials of the era to be cagey about the circumstances of his death, which was a black mark against those who ran professional cycling in Australia at the time. Why was his memory not properly preserved outside his hometown of Geelong?

In the end I decided that I would have faith in my belief that Mockridge's story was worth revisiting. There was a tale to tell a new generation about an unusual Australian. What other Australian athlete had given a first-hand account of an ordeal like the Tour de France without the assistance of a ghost writer or succumbing to self-service? What other Australian cyclist read the metaphysical poet John Donne? What other Australian cyclist remained the enigma that Mockridge was? How good was he? Could he have conquered Europe? Could he have won the Tour de France?

And then there was the nagging feeling, which I knew Irene shared, that the death could have been avoided if the bus driver had been sharper; if the race organisers had done a better job; if the busy corner had been staffed by a steward; if an official car with loudspeakers had been following the scratch bunch, broadcasting a warning...

September 13, 1958 was preliminary final day. Collingwood was playing North Melbourne at the Melbourne Cricket Ground. There was additional traffic into the city. There were races at Flemington.

People remember it as a terrible day because there was such a lot of form left in Russell Mockridge. And he was starting to emerge from his introspection. Irene told Lindy he was "just beginning to enjoy parties."

Were the race officials in the back bar of Kelly's Dandenong Rd pub, where the race started, getting their bets on for the day, instead of staffing the car with the loudspeaker, broadcasting a caution to motorists to look out for the bike riders, as Bob Mockridge claimed?

Australia in the 1950s was a zipped up world where most people left opinion making to newspaper columnists and politicians. There was a big funeral, but no one protested Mockridge's death.

On the 50th anniversary of his death, in a world intoxicated with in media, yet getting nothing much out of it except a wider girth, here was a chance to celebrate an Australian who stood up for his values and remind a new generation of cyclists that no matter how good you are on a bike, you'll never prevail against a bus.

And there was another point: to look out for yourself. Because on that day, no one was looking out for Russell Mockridge.

Chapter 3

The Reporter

MY TASK SHOULD be easy. Russell Mockridge wrote a book, *My World on Wheels*, published posthumously in 1960 by Scottish journalist John Burrowes and Irene Mockridge, about his cycling career.

He'd been a cub reporter on the *Geelong Advertiser* and he knew that he was in the box seat to report on doping, race fixing, promoters, the ups and downs of training and racing. He was frank about his doubts and insecurities, and there's a lot of melancholia evident in his writing. Between the ages of 20 and 30, when he wrote his book, he lacked the life skills to draw conclusions from his experiences.

But everything he'd learnt, he put to use in his description of his ride in the 1955 Tour de France. This was a heart-breaking, spirit-sapping 4,495-kilometre circuit of France, won for the third year in succession by the French champion Louis Bobet. The race brought to light the drug culture in professional cycling when French rider Jean Mallejac collapsed on Mount Ventoux in Provence in a delirium of amphetamines and dehydration.

Along with saturation-point coverage in the French press, the new medium of television brought the daily travails of the riders in the Tour to the attention of 15 million French viewers each night for the first time. Mockridge had curiosity value and his stamina was admired.

Australian cycling journalist Rupert Guinness found this tribute to Mockridge's ride in the French sports daily *l'Equipe* in 1955: "Mockridge is entitled to all our esteem. He showed all the qualities of the Australian people: strength of will, endurance and fortitude. So the gates of the 1956 Tour de France are wide open for him."

Russell Mockridge met his match on Stage 11 of the 1955 Tour de France between Marseilles and Avignon. His opponent was the 1,912-metre Mount Ventoux. Here is Mockridge's description from *My World on Wheels* of how he spent his 27th birthday on Monday, July 18, 1955. It is a rare first-person account of a dramatic day in 20th-century sport. It was the day that the world realised cyclists were putting their lives at risk by taking drugs to help them meet expectations. Mockridge used his words well to describe the unfolding drama and his part in it.

> Like all great operas, the Tour has its dramatic act. Every tour produces its moment of drama, and as the years pass these stories become revered legends.
>
> The scene was Mount Ventoux, the Via Dolorosa of the Tour. This day it looked just as I had imagined it would look in a Tour de France – a giant, smouldering 6,000-ft slagheap. I had seen pictures taken during previous Tours when it looked like this – not at all like the cool snowbound mountain we had climbed in the Tour of Vaucluse. [He had climbed the mountain that spring in the Tour du Vaucluse when it was in snow.]
>
> From the distance, the extinct volcano looked as though it was about to spark into life; its barren desert of a

summit glowed as though an inferno was raging inwardly. The prospect of being grilled by the heat on the harsh slopes of Ventoux stilled the eagerness of most of the riders in the early kilometres after leaving the old port of Marseilles. At 10am, shortly after the start, the temperature was well past the century and tar bubbles were popping on the road like jam in a preserving pan.

Even the Azureens and the Spaniards had complained of the heat in the morning and several team managers had pleaded with Goddet [tour director Jacques Goddet] to start the stage later in the day and miss some of the bludgeoning heat. He refused saying "the riders are paid for their job. They must get on with it. If it is too tough they will have to withdraw."

The great heat wave of the 1955 summer had already killed 200 people in Western Europe, but facts like this and the warning of the thermometer meant nothing to the fearless young Tour men. At Sanas, 59 kilometres, the younger riders were already feeling frisky and were stirring more speed from the sluggish brigade. We rolled on towards Ventoux, shimmering through the haze like a mammoth heap of ashes. I noticed Bobet, Gaul and some of the Italians taking occasional glances at the mountainous battleground. They wore frowning, apprehensive looks as David might have worn when he was on his way to meet Goliath.

Just before Malacene, a sleepy village which hugs the feet of the giant of Provence, we came upon the first of several rises which precede the mountain itself. These are not steep hills, and in normal circumstances would hardly require a smaller gear than used on a flat road. At first I could not understand why all the riders were passing me. I tried my smaller gears. Still they passed me. I sought out the lowest of my 10 gears, one good enough for the steepest mountains in Europe. But it was no good, I was being left behind and this was no mountain, just a gentle slope. Eventually I was pedalling as slowly as I had been on the last day of my first six-day race.

No longer were there riders around me. Already their many coloured vests were blending in with the grey-blue of the heat haze and disappearing into the distance. Finally, unable to pedal any farther, I dismounted. A farmer who had been spraying the others with water rushed up and aimed his hose at me. The chill of the water renewed my senses and I crammed my mouth full of loaf sugar. My Good Samaritan helped me on my machine and I was pedalling again. But not for long. The soaking from the hose dried within 200 yards, leaving me with as much life as an over-steamed cabbage. At the next farmhouse, there was no Samaritan with reviving water so I had to search for one.

I staggered into the kitchen of the small house and without saying a word the family went into action, like a team of veteran *soigneurs*. Madame sponged by face and the back of my neck with icy water while Monsieur fetched me a ladle of water to drink. They offered me some food but all I wanted was loaf sugar, as much as I could eat. Cube after cube I rammed into my mouth not caring about the way it clogged in my throat in a syrupy mess. The water soon washed it away, then I ate more sugar.

The two minutes in the shade out of the sun's blast gave me the recuperation I thought would never come. This time I could mount my machine without help and again I was on my way towards Ventoux. I would get over the torrid giant now because I felt much better. My spirit was coming back as fast as my strength, and I imagined myself like an army which has been almost defeated and then changed retreat into a successful counter-offensive.

Ahead of me the principal drama was being enacted. Jean Mallejac, third in a previous Tour, and a member of the French team, was making a crazy zig-zag across the road near the summit. With one foot firmly clamped to a pedal, he dragged his other foot on the road, continued for a few yards, then slumped in a heap by the roadside.

When Dr Dumas [tour doctor Pierre Dumas] arrived, he was almost dead and only a quick injection of soluble camphor and an oxygen mask brought some life back to his body. The doctor shouted for a police guard to keep everyone away from the stricken rider as he lay by the roadside, grey-faced, mouth foaming, eyes bulging. On his way to hospital Mallejac was in an absolute frenzy of delirium. The temperature was now more than 120 degrees [48.8°C].

But he was not the only one affected, although he was by far the worst. There were other riders collapsing or pedalling drunkenly on in the trial by fire. With some it was too much dope; with others it was the heat. Charly Gaul had to have an injection and Ferdi Kubler, the big Swiss who had attacked the Ventoux like a lunatic, at one point looked in a similar condition to Mallejac. But somehow he stayed on his machine past the summit, down the descent, only to collapse less than a mile from the finishing banner at Avignon.

Weeping, Kubler refused the help of his team-mate Bovay, who tried to assist him to pedal the last few yards. It took Ferdi over 20 minutes to snap out of his semi-comatose condition and pedal into Avignon, where he told the journalists, "Ferdi est trop charge. The Tour is finished for him. He is too sick, too old. Ferdi will never start again. He killed himself on the Ventoux."

On my own climb up the Ventoux I caught many of the riders who had left me earlier on the gentle slopes before the mountain proper. I lost count, after about 30, of the official cars that had to abandon their efforts to travel up the infernal mountain because of overheated engines.

When I passed Mallejac he was unconscious, slumped in the arms of Dr Dumas, and had an oxygen mask clamped over his haggard face.

Farther up the road Van Genechten, the tough little Belgian, was lying by the wayside in tears; others were silent as they slumped over their handlebars, some zig-zagging as they pedalled in a state of near collapse; and near Avignon I saw Kubler, in a bad way as he sat by the roadside.

Oh what a hellish way to spend a birthday.

Ahead of me, and ahead of everyone else on the ascent, was Bobet. He had raced up the mountain like a cycling salamander, impervious to heat and suffering. Not even the puncture which he had received on the descent could rob him of his ride to glory which ended with his entry into Avignon.

"A day like that takes years off our lives," he told journalists as he sagged from his machine in the old Provence town. His triumphal march had taken him to second place in classification, a brief five minutes behind his team-mate and lieutenant, Antonin Rolland, a man he could easily beat in the Pyrenees and in the time-trial stage. Bobet would now win the Tour for the third time.

Twelve years later in 1967, the English rider Tom Simpson keeled over on the climb up Mount Ventoux and died of heart failure. Post-mortem tests found both amphetamines and alcohol in his blood. His death moved authorities to introduce systematic drug testing.

Mockridge devoted a chapter of *My World on Wheels* to road racing and drugs, which were clearly in widespread use and, to some extent, endorsed by top riders such as Bobet. According to Mockridge the riders distinguished between dope and stimulants.

Dope, apparently, is the bomb that will send a rider romping home miles ahead of everyone else in the race and have such a bad after-effect that he will never ride well again.

Stimulants, according to Bobet, are the milder type of drugs in more common use which, if used wisely, have definite advantages without being harmful.

Mockridge classified Benzedrine as a stimulant and listed the possible contents of the "bomb" as amphetamines, caffeine, digitalis, cortisone, hormones, intravenous camphor, picritoxin and leptazol.

The prevailing wisdom was that, taken in conjunction with a preparation programme of vitamins, minerals and proteins, the stimulants would prevent exhaustion on a climb and keep the rider alert for the descent on a mountain pass where a misjudgement could mean death.

Here the stimulant appears justified. Whatever the rights and wrongs of their uses, it is standard practice for a rider in Europe who wants to take the sport seriously to find himself a trainer who is an expert in their use.

In a comment on the extent of drug use in Europe at the time, he said that most of the riders in the 1955 Rome–Naples–Rome race, when asked for a urine sample for a drug test, filled their sample bottles with tap water.

1950s French team manager Marcel Bidot said after his retirement that three quarters of the European riders of the era were using dope.

Mockridge was offered the "bomb" on many occasions, but refused; however, he believed his drink bottles were probably doctored at times by the *soigneurs*, or aides.

During the course [of six-day-races] bottles of various liquids are constantly being handed to you by your *soigneurs* and there is just not the time to insist on a written analysis of their contents. I had sufficient confidence in my *soigneurs* in these races to take what they gave me as I did not believe that they would knowingly give me something that would be harmful.

Mockridge finishes his chapter with words of wisdom from Belgian cyclist Alfred De Bruyne: "If I feel I cannot go on, I stop. It simply means that I have had enough. There is always a next time."

Mockridge concurred:

If I could not win a race without artificial stimulation, I would retire from cycling tomorrow. Also, to me, one of the most appealing things about being a professional athlete has been that I could live a clean, healthy life and develop fitness to such an extent that I could look forward to fit and healthy middle and old age. I cannot imagine anything more dreadful than to spend the later years of your life plagued by constant illness. I feel that the athlete who succumbs to the temptations of taking dope in his youth must surely pay some price later in life.

Mockridge did not win a prize in the 1955 Tour de France but he left a unique account of the bad old days of the Tour.

Mockridge stuffing sugar cubes down his throat is one image. Trainers and promoters prescribing amphetamines to get riders up and down a 2,000-metre volcanic plug in temperatures of 48.8°C is a much more sinister business.

Chapter 4

Read Between the Lines

THE PERSON WHO knew Russell Mockridge intimately, who shared his dreams and frustrations, is dead.

Irene Mockridge died in 2004, aged 75. She never gave any personal insights into her late husband that have been published.

She shunned the cycling community and she avoided interviews.

She lived a private life in a Victorian-era brick cottage in North Carlton. Before Russell's death, the family lived in Page Street, Middle Park, two streets from the beach, in a house they had started renovating. Irene moved with Lindy to East Malvern and then to Carlton in the 1970s, when Lindy started tertiary study at the University of Melbourne.

She travelled overseas when Lindy was seven, motoring around Europe and the UK in a Kombi van. She worked in the advertising industry, and in her 50s, travelled again to Europe with a view to living and working there. However, she couldn't get a work visa and so returned to Australia, completed an arts degree and worked for Australian Volunteers Abroad in the Solomon Islands.

She was an independent and capable woman. She followed the arts and was widely read.

Mockridge's parents were prominent Geelong citizens. Bob Mockridge rose through the ranks to become general manager of the Cheetham Salt Company, a Geelong institution. Bob's father was a well-regarded Geelong tailor.

His mother was Claire Riley, a descendant of the pioneer settler and explorer James Riley, a contemporary of the Polish explorer Paul Strzelecki, who was the first European to map Gippsland and eastern parts of the Great Dividing Range.

Claire had a blue-ribbon background. They lived in middle-class Newtown and sent their two boys to Geelong College for a private-school education. Russell and his older brother, Graham, spent their free time rabbiting in the Ceres hills and testing each other on weekend rides to Torquay, where their parents had a caravan. As school boys on heavy bikes, their record for the 22.5 kilometres from Geelong to Torquay was 30 minutes.

Australian Rules football was the sport of choice for Mockridge and the school, but short-sightedness stopped him playing. Unless he wore glasses, he would misjudge relatively easy marks and wearing glasses on the football field carried with it the risk of broken lenses in the face or eyes.

Geelong in the 1940s and 1950s was a town where people knew their place. The Western District graziers were cashed up on the back of the wool boom and social divisions were felt on many levels: Catholic–Protestant; boss–worker; Labor voter–Liberal voter–DLP voter; Catholic–Mason; public school–private school; unionist-non unionist; home owner–Housing Commission tenant. The only thing that Geelong people had in common was support for the Geelong Football Club.

The *Geelong Advertiser,* where Mockridge would start a journalism cadetship after getting his Leaving Certificate, was a conservative journal in the tradition of regional newspapers, whose owners saw things through a businesslike prism and generally endorsed a cautious social agenda as well as a political one.

Self consciousness about his pursuit of cycling rather than the traditional career paths of private-school educated, middle-class Geelong boys was evident in one comment he made about his old school.

> Geelong College has produced statesmen, writers, doctors and lawyers. Champion cricketers, athletes and oarsmen have also come from the school. But never previously a champion cyclist.

Mockridge's fairy-tale entry into cycling at 17 is well known. He turned up at a Geelong Cycling Club meet for an "out and back" on the Drysdale Road on a Sunday morning in June 1946, paid two-bob to enter and, because of his lack of experience, was given an 11-minute start over the scratch group in the 38.6 kilometre handicap event.

Before the halfway mark, he and fellow marker Don McGregor caught the limit man, who had a five-minute start on them, but after the turn he noticed that his companion was tiring.

Mockridge's style and substance was established that day when he politely asked McGregor, "I think I'll go on alone. Is that OK with you?"

Within a few months he was the next big thing in Australian cycling and within a year he was the Australian amateur road champion, set for the London Olympics of 1948.

He suffered gear failures in the London road race, but by 1950 was showing extraordinary track form by winning gold in the 1,000-metre sprint and 1,000-metre time trial at the Auckland Commonwealth Games. His time of 1 minute 13.4 seconds for the 1,000-metre time trial in 1950 was faster than that of Frenchman Jacques Dupont, who won the event at the 1948 Olympic Games.

In 1952, Mockridge won the Paris Amateur Grand Prix and, the next day, beat the best of Europe's professional cyclists in the Open Grand Prix. The amateur winner was invited to compete as a courtesy. He was not supposed to win. The next year the event became a race for professionals only after Mockridge became the first rider to win both divisions.

Next were the Helsinki Games in 1952 and two gold medals for Australia on the one day. Mockridge won the 1,000-metre time trial and set an Olympic record. He then teamed up with Lionel Cox and a tandem racing bike they had to assemble themselves to win through heats and finals and beat the pre-race favourites, the South African pair of Tommy Shardelow and Ray Robinson.

He turned professional a year after Helsinki and returned to Europe. Mockridge had mixed fortunes in 1953 and 1954 but found form in the first half of 1955 and caught attention by winning a major European six-day event, the Paris Six Day race, in an all-Australian team of Mockridge, Sid Patterson and Roger Arnold.

After winning the Tour du Vaucluse he was set for the personal and professional challenge of his life, the 1955 Tour de France. Starting sick and injured he was one of 69 from an original line-up of 130 to finish the 4,495-kilometre ordeal that started in Le Havre, on the English Channel, and took off clockwise around France, into Belgium and Luxembourg, through the French–Swiss Alps, along the Mediterranean coast and up the infamous Mount Ventoux, where he found his limit, before straying into the Pyrenees, and then up through the southwest region of France before a sprint into Paris.

Back in Australia, he was unbeatable on track or road.

He conquered the Warrnambool to Melbourne road race in 1956, setting a record that stood for 24 years. The next year he won the *Sun* Tour and the Tour of Tasmania and set the best time again in the Warrnambool to Melbourne race in a famous two-man handicap ride with training buddy Jim Taylor.

Mockridge's domination of Australian road cycling resulted in the *Sun* Tour being run as a handicap race in 1957. Despite the handicap, he and fellow backmarker George Goodwin closed the gap on the middle markers on the last day of the race that Mockridge won in a thrilling sprint.

He would probably have won several more *Sun* Tours but for a collision with the Clayton to Box Hill bus on September 13, 1958.

This much is well known in cycling circles. I felt that if I was going to do justice to Mockridge I had to take the story beyond a collection of statistics and cycling derring-do.

I first contacted Irene Mockridge in November 1996, aware that the 40th anniversary of her husband's death was approaching. I was working for the Leader suburban newspaper group and covering the southeastern suburbs. I tried to combine my paid job with my interest in the Mockridge story and suggested she back a campaign for some sort of marker or memorial at the corner where he was killed.

She was not keen on the idea, at all.

"It would be inappropriate to mark the spot. It's a bleak area that brings back bad memories," she said.

There were memorials to him: a circuit in Kings Park, Perth, and memorial gates at Centennial Park in Sydney, where he won his first Australian (amateur) road championship at 18 in 1947.

The clear message was that I could research this project without her. She wasn't going to help some suburban journalist get a story up.

She recommended Harry Gordon's book *Young Men in a Hurry* and said she believed Russell's own autobiography covered his life properly.

My only face-to-face meeting with Irene Mockridge was in October 1999 at a little coffee place called the Paragon Café in Rathdowne Street Carlton, near where she lived in Princes Street.

I got there early, could see no one of her age around, and sat at a table outside waiting for her to turn up. I was reading a cycling magazine. After about 10 minutes I checked the café again and found a woman annoyed that I was late. She gave me about five minutes before she shut down the conversation when I asked her to talk personally about Russell.

I took notes afterwards while her words were fresh in my mind.

She had no interest or sympathy for anything to do with cycling.

Even her husband copped a blast: "No one made them ride. The riders were just as stupid as the officials."

The accident was still painful to think about.

"I don't want to go over the accident or the inquest again. I'm not bitter, but it won't bring him back."

Then she unloaded on the officials behind the League of Victorian Wheelmen, who had organised the Tour of Gippsland.

It was dangerous to organise a bike race along Dandenong Road on a Saturday morning because of the high volume of traffic.

Cycling officials were incompetent and unprofessional.

They were "funny little men who liked bossing others about."

She called Russell's death a great tragedy and she used the imagery of a stone thrown into a pond to describe its impact.

"The ripples are still reaching into my life and others' lives."

Still angry? "I have to put it behind me. It's still very painful and upsetting to discuss. I don't want to go over the inquest again. It won't bring him back. In 1958 we were making plans to return to Europe in '59. We had happy times in Europe."

I asked her if she could talk about the private side of Russell, the part that few got to see. But this part of his memory was going to be kept intact, away from nosy reporters.

She called him reticent, shy, reluctant.

"Russell was a man of few words. After he won gold at Helsinki he sent me a telegram with one word – DID."

Irene was keen for the official memory to be preserved. He was the first Australian to win two gold medals in one day. That was the official version and that would have to do.

My lasting impressions: feisty, impatient, curt, bitter. She had utter contempt for cycling officialdom.

Mockridge's mate, Jim Taylor, said time didn't soften the loss for Irene Mockridge.

> She doted on him. She was in a car right behind. She was right there when it happened. She would have preferred Russell to be doing something else. Although she did appreciate the ability he had, I think the loss of Russell really turned her off the sport.

I can understand that life with a little baby girl would have been tough. The *Sun* newspaper ran a fund for him, £8,000 or so was raised. She never got much out of the court settlement, so she survived on her own. Pretty strong sort of woman, Irene.

Irene Mockride had health problems in her last 25 years, which reduced her quality of life. In 1979, she was diagnosed with breast cancer, which resulted in a mastectomy. In 1995, she had another breast removed. A cataract operation resulted in an allergic reaction to antibiotics and the loss of sight in one eye. She had emphysema and then kidney problems right at the end.

"All in all life wasn't great. Health issues became overwhelming towards the end," said Lindy in 2008.

Lindy portrays her mother as strong and resilient. While devastated by Russell's death, she put a life together for the two of them, and had a wide circle of friends who valued her sharp mind and her entertaining dinner parties.

September was the unlucky month in the family cycle.

"She would say to me 'watch out it's September'. Though they were married in September, she worried about things going bad in September," Lindy said.

Harry Gordon noted the closeness of Irene and Russell's relationship, perhaps hinting that Irene had too much ownership of one of the nation's golden boys.

Back in Australia [after the 1955 Tour] Russell Mockridge quickly dominated the local cycling scene. He had a brilliant track season, and was very soon the most feared man in road racing. During the 1956 Olympics he made a brief return to journalism; I got him a job writing for the Melbourne *Sun* about the cycle events. He tackled it earnestly, as he did most things, and after each day's racing he would sit with his pert wife for long periods composing his story. They were just about inseparable; whether swimming in Port Phillip Bay, writing, or delivering his copy, it seemed every time I saw Russell Mockridge in those days he was with his wife. Even when he was racing, with a newspaper stuffed under his singlet to keep out the cold, or training up and down Melbourne's Nepean Highway, she was just in front or just behind, in a small car.

In 2006 I made contact with Russell and Irene's daughter Lindy, to whom his autobiography is dedicated. Lindy is a teacher who works with children with behavioural problems. She lives in Melbourne with her partner Russell Smith, a criminologist, and her daughter Elinor from a previous marriage.

"You've got to read between the lines," she said, when I commented that her father did not reveal much of himself in his book.

"He was in a different class."

Yes, on several levels. He was a private-school boy in a blue-collar world of plumbers and dairy farmers. He'd grown up in class-conscious Geelong with conservative values. His mother was very proud of her pioneer heritage.

Russell, self acknowledged as shy, would have been struggling for conversation with his knock-about riding peers. But it's a mistake to see him as aloof or snobby, as some of the nicknames suggest.

He had a reputation for keeping his own counsel, and the individual nature of cycling, plus the enforced isolation of training rides, suited his personality.

His riding companions were ordinary blokes and the peloton delivers a fairly basic conversation. Russell, with his private-school background and aspirations for a higher calling in life, would not have fitted easily into this world. He may have been uncomfortable with blokey, locker-room language. He may have just wanted to be left alone to get on with what he did best – ride a racing bike faster than anyone else.

His shyness was pathological. At one stage in his book he put himself in the persona of Professor Henry Higgins, the George Bernard Shaw character who brought Eliza Doolittle to class-conscious English society in *My Fair Lady*, saying he was happiest spending his evenings in the silence of his room, "in an atmosphere as restful as an undiscovered tomb."

In one passage he wrote that "having to mix with people other than my closest personal friends has always found me affected by tension and the resulting loss of nervous energy has frequently affected my physical ability."

Despite this shyness Mockridge did form strong friendships. To his gold medal tandem partner, Lionel Cox, Mockridge was a "beautiful man."

"He was a gentleman through and through. We were two different blokes, we came from different backgrounds, but we got on well together. As a cyclist he was a natural."

Cox, who was 78 in 2008, fronts up at the Tempe cycle track in inner Sydney two nights a week to coach young riders. He has given a lot to cycling. He's from the school that worked hard for everything they got. His fare to Helsinki was partly paid for through a raffle among his work mates at the Sydney fruit and vegetable markets. He rewarded their faith in him with a gold and silver medal.

Makeshift crosses dot the highways of Australia, marking the spot where people have died in vehicle collisions. They bring home the personal cost of the road toll and are potent reminders of what happens when fast-moving, heavy metal vehicles hit other objects, moving and stationary. Officials for many years tried, stupidly, to ban these memorials. They interfered with road verge mowing and grading schedules.

The markers convey the numerical weight and randomness of the road toll. They are usually in very plain locations, places not memorable for any other feature. These are the aesthetics of death on the road.

The intersection of Clayton and Dandenong roads, where Mockridge died, is a place so ordinary, so unlovely, so much a functional intersection of commuter and business traffic, that it was an insult to Mockridge's memory, in his widow's view, that his life should be remembered at this prosaic place.

Another view is that the unfulfilled promise and talent that was crushed under the back wheels of a bus that sunny Saturday morning should be remembered, where it happened, to remind cyclists and motorists that the price of life is eternal watchfulness, and that an error of judgement can cost you, or someone else, a life.

Russell Mockridge should be commemorated in a prestigious way – the Melbourne Park velodrome is named after a Chinese white-goods company, not a cycling great. The State Cycling Centre and velodrome at Northcote, built for the 2006 Commonwealth Games, is named after a cycling official. Both Mockridge and his main rival in Australia, Sid Patterson, should be remembered in a lasting tribute. If naming rights are not available, an artistic tribute should be commissioned.

Because of his status, and to remind us of the dangers of doing battle on the bitumen, his life should also be marked at the crossroads where it ended.

Chapter 5

On Tour

THERE ARE SCORES of newspaper articles and sports book chapters on Russell Mockridge, so I took his widow's advice and researched as many as I could find. They all tell the story of the "Geelong Flyer," or "Mocka," or "Wrong Way Mockridge," or the "China Doll," or "Little Lord Fauntleroy"; it's the story of a 180cm, 77.5 kilogram chronically near-sighted boy from Geelong, who won a 38.6 kilometre (24 mile) Geelong Cycling Club event on a non-racing bike at his first outing in 1946 and, within the space of a year, became the Australian amateur road champion, with a berth on the boat to London for the 1948 Olympics. Then it becomes a story about self-doubt and confusion, a painful and embarrassingly public search for personal direction and meaning in a world that expects simple messages from its sporting heroes and not introspective soul-searching. Then he meets Irene, who becomes the love of his life, and they have a baby, Melinda, and he's happy and we're happy, and he rides, virtually solo, the Tour de France, in a sort of 4,495-kilometre religious scourging, and then comes back to Australia, finds his feet, and is run over by a bus just after the start of a professional road race.

The best account of this life can be found in Harry Gordon's *Young Men in a Hurry*, which correctly puts Mockridge in the company of John Landy, Herb Elliot, Peter Thomson, Ken Rosewall, Lew Hoad, John Konrads, Merv Lincoln, Hec Hogan, Marjorie Jackson, Shirley Strickland and Betty Cuthbert. This was Gordon's tribute to the athletes of the 1950s, when Australian sporting ability was demonstrated through individual achievement, and at the "Friendly Games", the 1956 Melbourne Olympics, where war-weary Europe became enchanted with Australian hospitality and charm.

Gordon himself was a young man in a hurry, notably dedicating his 1961 book to his family, "without whom this book would have been finished in half the time." His chapter on Mockridge is titled "The Man on the Outside", capturing the loner in the athlete.

Max and Reet Howell wrote a good piece on Mockridge in their 1988 book *Aussie Gold* and, more recently, Rupert Guinness dissected his 1955 Tour de France achievement in his 2003 *Aussie Aussie Aussie, Oui! Oui! Oui!*, which looked at Australians in 100 years of the Tour de France.

Did these writers miss anything – I have to ask myself at this point. Is there new light I can shed on his life, any personal insights that have eluded others?

Part of the answer lay in going on the road with the man himself and sharing his perspective of the highs and lows of the 42nd Tour de France as described in *My World on Wheels*.

Mockridge never planned to win the Tour. His ambition was to finish the race and honour the achievement of his hero, Hubert Opperman, the last Australian to complete the race, 24 years earlier, in 1931. Mockridge's manager, Gino Bambagiotti,

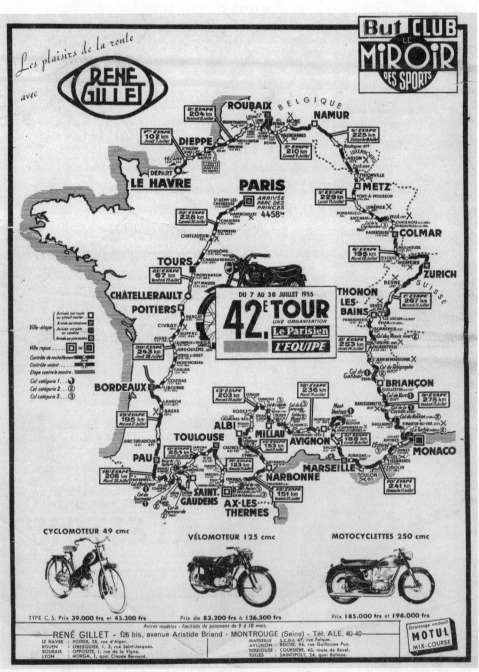

Route of 1955 Tour De France
Reproduced with permission of the Mockridge family.

wanted him to try for a stage finish because that meant fame and future contracts on the European circuit.

Mockridge had crashed during a training run a week before the start of the race and badly gashed his knee. He and fellow Australian John Beasley were also suffering from food poisoning on the eve of the race, which they put down to a celebratory seafood feast at the seaport of Le Havre, where the race started.

Mockridge was anxious about his preparation for the race. He and Beasley were in the Luxembourg-International team, a mixed group of riders at a time when the race was run on national team lines, and it became clear early on that while they were welcome to share the workload through the day, any prize money would not be shared with the Australians. Mockridge wrote in his book:

> Contrary to my expectations, there were no tactical discussions when our team gathered at meal times. Nicholas Frantz, our manager, obviously felt that John and I were only present to make up team numbers. We were a team only in that we wore the same colours. Otherwise the Germans, the Austrians and John and I were excluded from the plans made by the four Luxembourgers who were the force of the squad.

The race favourite was Louis Bobet, the two-time winner of the Tour and reigning world road champion, riding for a history-making third successive win.

Cycling journalist Rupert Guinness wrote that Bobet and the French team were favoured to win.

Besides being in great form [having won the Paris–Roubaix] the French national team – including his brother Jean – was extremely strong and dedicated to him. One of his teammates, Antonin Rolland, became the caretaker wearer of the yellow jersey for two weeks. He surrendered it to Bobet in the Pyrenees during the 206 km 18th stage from St Gaudens to Pau. The 18th stage was the decisive stage won by the Belgian, Jean Brankart, who finished second overall, while third overall was a 21-year-old Tour revelation, Luxembourg's Charly Gaul.

The French team would dominate the race, but it was Mockridge's Luxembourg-International team captain, the "Angel of the Mountain", Charly Gaul, who unexpectedly challenged their supremacy.

The Cast

Russell Mockridge: Luxembourg-International team rider
John Beasley: 1951 Australian professional road champion and member of Luxembourg team
Gino Bambagiotti (Bamba): friend and manager to Russell Mockridge
Nicholas Frantz: Luxembourg team manager; 1927 and 1928 Tour de France winner
Charly Gaul: the "Angel of the Mountain"; Luxembourg-International team captain
Willy Kemp: Luxembourg team rider
Jean Brankart: Belgian rider
Louison Bobet: 1953 and 1954 Tour winner; French team leader. Reigning world road champion

Antonin Rolland: French team rider; second in command to Bobet

Raphael Geminiani: Italian-born French rider

Jean Mallejac: French rider

Roger Hassenforder: French rider

Jean Bobet: French rider; brother of Louison

Miguel Poblet: Spanish rider

Andre Leducq: 1930 and 1932 Tour winner; influential sports journalist

Jacques Goddet: race director

Pierre Dumas: 1955 Tour doctor

Ferdi Kubler: Swiss rider; 1950 Tour winner

Wout Wagtmans: Dutch rider

Pasquale Fornara: leading Italian rider

Stage 1: Le Havre–Dieppe, 102 km

Only a few kilometres after the mass start of 130 riders, Mockridge pondered whether the Tour would be better named the Sprint de France. He suffered a puncture at 60 kilometres, just as the field was sprinting to catch a breakaway led by Miguel Poblet of Spain. Mockridge finished the stage in 126th place, Beasley was two places behind Mockridge. There was then a 12.5-kilometre time trial for the teams around the Dieppe waterfront. The Luxembourg team finished 9th. It was an inauspicious start for Mockridge and Beasley.

I was dispirited that first night at having finished so far back. Never had I dreamed of winning the Tour but I had not expected to be last either. I could not get over the fact that we had lost ten minutes in our chase. Surely they could not keep up such a pace for 3,000 miles?

The stage was won by Poblet in 2 hours 39 minutes and 31 seconds. He also became the Tour leader and first Spanish rider to wear the *maillot jaune*.

Stage 2: Dieppe–Roubaix, 204 km

Mockridge kept near the leaders over the road to Roubaix, which he had ridden in the Paris–Roubaix or "Hell of the North", earlier in the year. He improved his position in Stage 2 and finished in 16th position, just under two minutes behind stage winner Antonin Rolland, the number two rider in the French team. Beasley's difficulties with a stomach upset were evident in his placing – 123rd, only four off the tail.

Rolland won the stage in 5 hours and 54 minutes, but Wout Wagtmans (Netherlands) took the lead, followed by Fred De Bruyne (Belgium), Eugene Telotte (France) and Antonin Rolland.

Stage 3: Roubaix–Namur, 210 km

In the third stage, Louis Bobet made his first bid for victory. According to Mockridge there was no finesse or tactic behind it.

> All he did was to wait until the field was rolling along at top speed, and then go faster himself. He dashed out about 50 metres in front of the field and stayed there, holding off the attempts of more than a hundred men to catch him.

Bobet won the stage and entered the general classification in 4th position. He stayed in the top ten of the general classification for the rest of the race.

Mockridge was exhausted at the end of the day.

We looked like a string of Belgian miners coming up from the coalface when we arrived in Namur, having spent a deal of the journey bouncing along the foot and cycle paths skirting the cobbled roads.

The finish at Namur is a Tour organiser's delight. The citadel in which the race finishes is at the top of a 1,000 ft mountain. When there is such a hill at the end of a stage that has been like one long sprint, it completely shatters the field. Riders struggle home in ones and twos, many minutes separating the leaders from the tail enders.

Charly Gaul was expected to challenge Bobet in the finish, but failed to find form, finishing in 33rd place, behind Mockridge.

It was on this stage that John Beasley was forced to quit the Tour. Both he and Mockridge were dealing with vomiting and diarrhoea. Beasley fell halfway through the day and then punctured. He found himself last in the field battling illness and, finally, a hot and strong headwind. He did not finish within the time limit and was eliminated. Mockridge lost his only confidant in the team.

Mockridge finished in 29th place, 11.5 minutes behind Bobet, who won the stage in 6 hours 37 minutes and 39 seconds. The overall leader was Wagtmans, followed by Rolland, Jean Robic (France) and Louis Bobet in 4th position.

Stage 4: Namur–Metz, 225 km

The fourth day had the riders in three countries. From Namur in Belgium, the course went through Luxembourg and then into eastern France to Metz.

The day started on a low for the Luxembourg-International team after their manager, Nicolas Frantz, made it clear at breakfast that the hope of the side, Charly Gaul, was not living up to expectations.

However, the stage proved a winner for the Luxembourg group after Willy Kemp joined a breakaway group and finished 11 minutes ahead of the pack.

> Willy won the stage in quite an artful fashion. Near Metz the race passed over a bridge, divided for two lanes of traffic, but like every other stretch of roadway it was closed for the Tour. As he approached the bridge with the breakaway group Willie sneaked off from the rear and cut up the left lane of the bridge while the others plodded along the right side line.

Mockridge finished in 29th position along with Bobet and again ahead of Gaul. Kemp rode the distance in 6 hours 41 minutes and 7 seconds. Rolland, who was part of the breakaway group, took over the yellow jersey, Wagtmans went to 2nd place, followed by Robic and Louis Bobet. Rolland's riding was impressive. He had a 13 minute lead over his captain.

Stage 5: Metz–Colmar 229 km

The first climbing stage through the Vosges mountains opened to see Mockridge in agony. A night's rest had brought no recovery from injuries and illness and every part of him ached.

> Even the slightest pressure on the pedals brought pain and I cursed the eager beavers who were prancing about at the front of the peloton trying to urge more speed and stimulating a breakaway movement which would mean the usual rearguard action to chase them. How wonderful

Cross-section map of 1955 Tour de France showing elevations.
Reproduced with permission of the Mockridge family.

it was when an escape movement was thwarted and there was a slight respite in the speed. But it never lasted for long. There was always someone wanting to escape to glory and maybe a step up in the classification ladder.

Despite his suffering, self-doubt and concern about inadequate preparation, he finished the day 12th, his best placing of the Tour and nine minutes behind the stage winner, Roger Hassenforder of France, who won the day in 5 hours 57 minutes and 54 seconds.

Rolland was the Tour leader, followed by team-mates Roger Hassenforder and Jean Bobet. Wagtmans was 4th and Louis Bobet was in 6th position

Stage 6: Colmar–Zurich 195 km

Day six opened like a scene from a battlefield.

I could see that I was not the only one suffering in the Tour. Bandages were becoming prominent on grazed knees and elbows and faces were looking more drawn and haggard.

This was meant to be the Swiss champion, Ferdi Kubler's day. The sight of the Swiss border energised the big rider and he took off, "superman-fashion", so he could be the first into Zurich, his hometown.

Kubler, the 1950 Tour winner, resisted his pursuers until the French team manager, Marcel Bidot, ordered the French sprinter, Andre Darrigade to catch him. Darrigade and a group of chasers caught Kubler near Zurich and checked him by refusing to share the pace. The French rider took the benefit of the slipstream on Kubler's wheel and then rushed past him in the sprint finish.

Mockridge finished the ride into the Swiss capital in 14th place. Darrigade's time was 4 hours 32 minutes and 14 seconds.

The general classification positions did not change. Rolland retained the yellow jersey followed by Hassenforder, Wagtmans and Pasquale Fornara of Italy. Louis Bobet remained in 6th position.

Stage 7: Zurich–Thonon les Bains 267 km

Mockridge and the other riders could see the challenges that lay ahead in the Swiss Alps. The ride to Lake Geneva was wet and muddy but the real challenge loomed in the distance, with three mountains to climb.

> The mechanics were busier than usual that night hammering big cog wheels on our rear wheels and rearranging our chain wheel sizes to give us a greater selection of small gears for the next day. We would need them.

Stage 7 was won by Jos Hinsen of the Netherlands in 7 hours 22 minutes and 1 second. Mockridge finished in 26th place. Wim van Est of the Netherlands stole the yellow jersey for the day. In 2nd place was Rolland followed by Hassenforder. Louis Bobet dropped to 9th.

Stage 8: Thonon les Bains–Briancon, 253 km

On the first Alpine stage, Charly Gaul, the star of the Luxembourg team, finally found his form and won the stage by 15 minutes. The three big climbs were over the Col les Aravis (1,498 metres), Col du Telegraphe (1,670 metres) and the Col du Galibier (2,556 metres). Gaul was the first over each mountain, giving Frantz the reassurance that he had a winner in his stable and throwing down the gauntlet to the French.

Bobet could not find a group to launch a counter-offensive and Gaul finished in Briancon 15 minutes ahead of the next group, which included Bobet. In one day, Gaul went from 37th place to 3rd in the general classification. Bobet was in 6th position.

There was now anxiety in the French camp about Gaul and the Italian rider Pasquale Fornara, also ahead of Bobet in classification. But according to the French manager Marcel Bidot, "There is still the Ventoux and then the Pyrenees and if Charly rides as well on these there is still the time trial."

Mockridge finished in 59th place. This was the stage where Mockridge's stoic performance caught the eye of 1930 and 1932 Tour winner Andrew Leducq, who was writing a daily column in *l'Equipe*.

"I did not have much time for sprinters in the Tour, but if Mockridge finishes, I will shake his hand as warmly as I shake that of the winner," he wrote in his daily column.

Fourteen days later, in Paris, Leducq would honor his promise and pay a personal tribute to the Australian sprinter who was showing great ability as an endurance athlete.

Gaul won the stage in 7 hours 42 minutes and 55 seconds. Rolland regained the yellow jersey, followed by van Est and Gaul in 3rd place. Louis Bobet sat in 6th spot.

Stage 9: Briancon–Monaco 275 km

Day 9 gave Mockridge a lift as he was riding over familiar territory and, at the end of the day, Irene and Lindy would be waiting in Monaco and they could all enjoy a rest day together. But there were 275 kilometres to ride and nearly 7,000 metres to climb before the rewards could be taken and, in the rain,

63 of the 98 riders fell on the descent from the Col du Vasson (1,700 metres). Among the victims were Mockridge and Gaul, who had won the three previous mountain stages before crashing on the way down Col du Vasson.

The slippery roads on this longest Tour day also claimed most of the support teams and media on motorbikes.

The stage was won by the French team rider Raphael Geminiani in 8 hours 15 minutes and 50 seconds. At the end of the 9th stage and as the Tour neared the halfway mark Frenchman Antonin Rolland was in first position and wearing the yellow jersey confidently, Pasquale Fornara of Italy was 2nd, Bobet moved into 3rd position and Gaul was 4th.

Gaul had stamped his name on the climbers title.

Mockridge could tell from the look on Irene's face when she met him that he was looking the worse for wear. But if he could finish it would make a difference to the size of his contracts in Europe and Australia and no Australian had completed the course since Hubert Opperman in 1931. He finished in 76th spot, 52 minutes behind the stage winner.

> And if I did not finish? It was a distinct possibility. I was not riding myself in like other riders who seemed to be going better as the days wore on. But surely there could be no worse hell than the past nine days. And if there was not – I would reach Paris.

Stage 10: Monaco–Marseilles 240 km

The three-day transition stage between the Alps and the Pyrenees was across the Massif Central and deceptively hard.

According to Rupert Guiness, "There are few giant mountains to tackle but the passage is littered with repetitive ups and downs, many long, twisting and steep. Adding to the mix is the oppressive summer heat and the hectic race pace caused by opportunistic riders not in overall contention trying to snare a stage win."

Mockridge was boosted by the time with Irene and Lindy and got a wave from them as the Tour passed through Nice along the Promenade des Anglais. However, the rest day had not been enough to revive his fortunes. Mockridge finished in 71st spot. The stage was won by Lucien Lazarides of France in 6 hours 45 minutes and 12 seconds. The leading group remained intact: Rolland, Fornara, Bobet and Gaul.

Stage 11: Marseilles–Avignon, 198 km

Monday, July 18, 1955, was Mockridge's 27th birthday and the day that Mount Ventoux, the Giant of Provence, would shatter the field. The climb up the 1,912 metre-high mountain triggered revelations about doping in the Tour when the French rider Jean Mallejac collapsed from a combination of amphetamines and dehydration.

Mallejac's captain delivered a notable victory on the stage, lifting him to 2nd place in the overall classification behind team leader Rolland. The leaders were Rolland, Bobet, Fornara and Jean Brankart of Belgium. Gaul was pushed to 5th spot.

Bobet won the ride over the airless mountain and the stage in 5 hours 42 minutes and 32 seconds. Mockridge finished in 59th place from a total of 79 riders who finished the day.

Stage 12: Avignon–Millau 240 km

The ordeal on Mount Ventoux had taken its toll and the departure of the Swiss rider Ferdi Kubler left a big gap in the peloton. The pace for the next four days was less demanding but it was still racing. There was another mountain stage in this day's ride, Col du Minier (1,270 metres), won by Louis Caput of France. The day was won by Alessandro Fantini of Italy in 6 hours 53 minutes and 50 seconds. Mockridge came in last in 76th place. Gaul was in 8th position. The leader group was Rolland, Bobet, Fornara and Brankart.

Stage 13: Millau–Albi, 205 km

Mockridge was starting to lose condition through a combination of fatigue, tired limbs and saddle blisters. The ordeal on Mount Ventoux had left him exhausted. Daan de Groot of the Netherlands won the stage in 5 hours 52 minutes and 41 seconds. Mockridge was placed 69th of the remaining 75 riders, 24 minutes behind the stage winner.

The leaders were unchanged: Rolland, Bobet, Fornara and Brankart. Gaul remained 8th.

Stage 14: Albi–Narbonne, 156 km

There was another mountain to climb, La Fontasse, but it was small by European standards at 676 metres. On top of saddles sores Mockridge was struggling with his breathing by this stage of the race. He finished last in 75th position and outside the time limit and faced elimination. That night he underwent a chest X-ray and was diagnosed with bronchitis. However, he was reprieved and the officials declared that he completed the stage "under extreme difficulties" and so was allowed to keep racing. The stage was won by Louis Caput in 4 hours 12 minutes and 5 seconds.

The top four was unchanged. Gaul fell to 9th spot.

Stage 15: Narbonne–Ax les Thermes, 151 km

The drama on the stage to Ax-les-Thermes was provided by the spectacular fall of Nello Lauredi, a *domestique* in the French team, who failed to take a bend in the descent from the Col de Chioula (1,449 metres) and sailed off the road at about 80 km/h into a ravine, breaking his collar bone. The stage winner was Luciano Pezzi of Italy who finished in 4 hours 32 minutes and 53 seconds. Mockridge finished 48th from 74 survivors. The French remained dominent. Gaul held on in 9th position.

Stage 16: Ax les Thermes–Toulouse, 123 km

This was the beginning of the assault on the Pyrenees, with climbs over the Col d'Aspin, Col de Peyresourde, Col de Tourmalet, Col du Soulor and Col d'Aubisque ahead of them. Mockridge noted the total of these five climbs to be 8,356 metres almost the height of Mount Everest. Mockridge was becoming more valuable to the Luxembourg team, who were down to five, half the number that started. The job of the remaining riders was to support Gaul in every possible way. To shelter him on the flat so he had reserves for the hills, and to give him a wheel should he puncture, so he didn't lose time. The day was won by Rik Van Steenbergen of Belgium in 2 hours 57 minutes and 9 seconds. Louis Bobet was sitting just under 5 minutes behind team-mate Rolland at the start of the second mountain stage that would settle the Tour.

Stage 17: Toulouse–St Gaudens, 249 km

The "Angel of the Mountain" launched his attack early in the day and was first up the Col d' Aspin (1,489 metres) and Col de Peyresourde (1,569 metres), but Charly Gaul was chased by Bobet and his supporters, and finally caught on the descent of Col de Peyresourde.

However a puncture deprived Bobet of a stage victory and the day went to Gaul who came in at 7 hours 31 minutes and 31 seconds. Gaul finished 1 minute and 24 seconds ahead of Bobet, but the French leader's time had come and he took the yellow jersey from team-mate Antonin Rolland. In 3rd place was Pasquale Fornara and Charly Gaul moved into 4th position in the overall classification. Bobet announced that he had "seized the race."

Stage 18: St Gaudens–Pau, 206 km

Bobet maintained his lead despite another attack from Gaul. However, Mockridge's team-mate moved to 3rd place in the overall classification at the end of the day.

> Again there was rain and cool breezes blowing off the rugged barren mountains on the second and toughest day in the Pyrenees. And again Charly attacked. But the new yellow jersey winner, Bobet, was this day his equal on the climbs and the pair took off together on the Soulor. Surprise of the day was the failure of the Italian, Pasquale Fornara. He cracked on the climb on the Aubisque (1,709 metres) and finished 11 minutes behind Charly and Louison. Charly now took over third place and Fornara slipped to seventh.

The stage winner was Jean Brankart of Belgium, who finished in 6 hours 39 minutes and 39 seconds. Mockridge finished 52nd in the remaining field of 70. The leaders were Bobet, Rolland, Gaul and Brankart. With the climbing done, Bobet had six minutes on Rolland and over seven on Gaul and Brankart.

Ils sont partis 130...

EQUIPE DE FRANCE

(Maillot bleu de France, ceinture blanc et rouge ; casquette blanche, bande bleu, blanc et rouge.)

1. BOBET Louis.
2. BOBET Jean.
3. DARRIGADE André.
4. DOTTO Jean.
5. FORESTIER Jean.

6. GAUTHIER Bernard.
7. GEMINIANI Raphaël.
8. MAHE François.
9. MALLEJAC Jean.
10. ROLLAND Antonin.

EQUIPE DE BELGIQUE

(Maillot bleu nattier, ceinture noire, jaune et rouge ; casquette blanche, bande noir, jaune et rouge.)

11. ADRIAENSSENS Jean.
12. BRANKART Jean.
13. CLOSE Alexandre.
14. COUVREUR Hilaire.
15. DE BRUYNE Alfred.

16. IMPANIS Jean.
17. OCKERS Jean.
18. SORGELOOS Edgard.
19. VAN GENECHTEN Richard.
20. VAN STEENBERGEN Henri.

EQUIPE D'ESPAGNE

(Maillot gris perle, ceinture rouge et jaune ; casquette blanche, bande rouge et jaune.)

21. ALOMAR Francisco.
22. BOTELLA Salvador.
23. COMPANY Gabriel.
24. GELABERT Antonio.
25. LORONO Jesus.

26. MASSIP Francisco.
27. MATEO Jesus.
28. MORALES José.
29. POBLET Miguel.
30. RUIZ Bernardo.

EQUIPE DE GRANDE-BRETAGNE

(Maillot blanc, ceinture noire, écusson Union Jack ; casquette blanche, bande noire.)

31. BEDWELL Dane.
32. HOART Tony.
33. JONES Stan.
34. KREBS Fred.
35. MAITLAND Robert.

36. MITCHELL Ken.
37. PUSEY Bernard.
38. ROBINSON Brian.
39. STEEL Ian.
40. WOOD Bevis.

EQUIPE DE HOLLANDE

(Maillot blanc, ceinture bleu et rouge ; casquette blanche, bande rouge et bleu.)

41. DE GROOT Daan.
42. HAAN Piet.
43. HINSEN Joseph.
44. NOLTEN Jan.
45. VAN BREENEN Johan.

46. VAN DONGEN Wies.
47. VAN EST Wim.
48. VOORTING Adrian.
49. VOORTING Gerrit.
50. WAGTMANS Wout.

EQUIPE D'ITALIE

(Maillot vert, ceinture blanc et rouge ; casquette blanche, bande vert, blanc et rouge.)

51. ASTRUA Giancarlo.
52. BAROZZI Danilo.
53. BENEDETTI Gino.
54. BERTOGLIO Eugenio.
55. COLETTO Agostino.

56. FANTINI Alessandro.
57. FORNARA Pasquale.
58. GUIDICI Pietro.
59. MONTI Bruno.
60. PEZZI Luciano.

The team lists of the 1955 Tour de France.

EQUIPE DU LUXEMBOURG-MIXTE

(Maillot rouge, ceinture blanc et bleu ;
casquette blanche, bande rouge et bleu.)

61. GAUL Charly.
62. GELHAUSSEN Francis.
63. KEMP Willy.
64. MORN Nicolas.
65. KAIN Alfred.
66. SCHNEIDER Kurt.
67. MUELLER Heintz.
68. PANKOKE Gunther.
69. BEASLEY John.
70. MOCKRIDGE Russell.

EQUIPE DE SUISSE

(Maillot rouge, croix blanche ;
casquette blanche, bande rouge.)

71. BAUVAY Jacquy.
72. CLERICI Carlo.
73. CROCI-TORTI Emilio.
74. GRAF Rolf.
75. HOLLENSTEIN Hans.
76. HUBER Marcel.
77. KUBLER Ferdi.
78. MEILI Otto.
79. RUDOLF Ernst.
80. SCHELLEMBERG Max.

EQUIPE DE L'ILE-DE-FRANCE

(Maillot mi-bleu, mi-rouge ;
casquette blanche, bande bleue.)

81. BARONE Nicolas.
82. BOBER Stanislas.
83. CAPUT Louis.
84. DACQUAY Jean.
85. DIOT Maurice.
86. FORLINI Dominique.
87. HOORELBECKE Raymond.
88. SIGUENZA Francis.
89. TELOTTE Eugène.
90. VITRE Isaac.

EQUIPE NORD-EST-CENTRE

(Maillot orange, bande blanche ;
casquette blanche, bande orange.)

91. ANZILE Ugo.
92. BAUVIN Gilbert.
93. BUCHONNET Roger.
94. CIELESKA Jean-Marie.
95. COHEN Max.
96. HASSENFORDER Roger.
97. REISSER Raymond.
98. SCODELLER Gilbert.
99. STABLINSKI Jean.
100. WALKOWIAK Roger.

EQUIPE DE L'OUEST

(Maillot blanc, parements rouges ;
casquette blanche.)

101. BOUVET Albert.
102. BULTEL Bernard.
103. COLETTE Claude.
104. LE BER Claude.
105. PICOT Fernand.
106. QUENTIN Maurice.
107. ROBIC Jean.
108. RUBY Pierre.
109. SITEK Henri.
110. VARNAJO Robert.

EQUIPE DU SUD-EST

(Maillot violet, ceinture blanche ;
casquette blanche, bande violette.)

111. DELEDDA Adolphe.
112. DI CARO Armand.
113. LAUREDI Nello.
114. LAZARIDES Apo.
115. LAZARIDES Lucien.
116. MIRANDO José.
117. MOLINERIS Pierre.
118. REMY Raoul.
119. TEISSEIRE Lucien.
120. VITETTA Vincent.

EQUIPE DU SUD-OUEST

(Maillot havane, ceinture verte ;
casquette blanche, bande verte.)

121. AGUT Philippe.
122. BERGAUD Louis.
123. DESBATS Robert.
124. DUPONT Jacques.
125. DUPRE André.
126. FERNANDEZ Marcel.
127. GAY Georges.
128. HUOT Valentin.
129. LAMPRE Maurice.
130. VIVIER Jacques.

Stage 19: Pau–Bordeaux, 195 km

This day took the 70 survivors out of the Pyrenees and through the wine country of Bordeaux. There was little activity and no change in the classifications. Mockridge finished in 40th position. The stage was won by Wout Wagtmans of the Netherlands in 5 hours 15 minutes and 38 seconds. The leadership group had cemented around Bobet, Rolland, Gaul and Brankart.

Stage 20: Bordeaux–Poitiers, 243 km

Mockridge noted that on Stage 20 the offensives and counter offensives were over. Only tomorrow's second-last stage, the time trial, could affect the classification. Jean Forestier of France took line honours in 7 hours 24 minutes and 12 seconds. Mockridge finished in 22nd spot. The top four remained intact.

Stage 21: Chatellerault–Tours, 68.6 km

The time trial was won by Jean Brankart of Belgium who completed the distance in 1 hour 39 minutes and 51 seconds and he moved into 2nd position in the overall classification. Bobet finished 3rd in the stage, just under two minutes behind Brankart, but he had enough credit in the bank to concede the time. Mockridge finished 55th in the remaining pack of 69. On the penultimate day the leaders were Bobet, Brankart, Gaul and Fornara.

Stage 22: Tours–Paris, 229 km

For three weeks Mockridge had suffered and strained through 4,495 kilometres of French countryside. Paris, and the end of the ordeal, was in sight. The day belonged to

GAUL Charles (22 ans). — Ses extraordinaires dispositions pour la montagne peuvent en faire un nouveau « Vietto 1934 ».

Charles Gaul, Captain of the Luxembourg International Team who Russell helped into 3rd Place in the 1955 Tour de France.

Reproduced with permission of the Mockridge family.

KEMP Willy (30 ans). — Un bon élément du Tour de France.

MORN Nicolas (26 ans). — De grandes qualités de fond.

GELHAUSEN Francis (29 ans). — Un élément de soutien.

SCHNEIDER Kurt (26 ans). Décontracté mais courageux.

Luxembourg International team members of 1955 including two Australians, Russell Mockridge and John Beasley.

Reproduced with permission of the Mockridge family.

BEASLEY John (26 ans). — Surprit dans le Dauphiné.

MOCKRIDGE Russell (26 ans). Pur sprinter devenu vrai routier.

Miguel Poblet, who won the stage, but the Tour went to Bobet, who was greeted by 35,000 fans when he entered the Park de Princes track to become the first person to win the Tour three times in a row.

Mockridge rode into the stadium in the main group, 14 seconds behind Poblet.

> The yell that exploded from the overflow crowd as we burst through the tunnel and on to the pink concrete was like a giant volcano exploding. One and a half laps around the 454-metre track and the 1955 Tour de France had concluded.

"The Tour is dead," Mockridge wrote, "Long live the Tour."

The race had been run at an average speed of 34.4 km/h. Total prize money for the race was FF 36 million.

First position went to Louis Bobet in the time of 130 hours 29 minutes and 26 seconds. Second was Jean Brankart, 4 minutes 53 seconds behind the leader. Third was Charly Gaul, the rider who Mockridge had protected and helped, 11 minutes and 30 seconds behind the leader. Gaul also won "King of the Mountains". The points winner was Stan Ockers of Belgium.

Mockridge finished 64th in the general classification, 4 hours 14 minutes and 46 seconds behind Louis Bobet and five off the tail.

His ride had caught the attention of the French media. He was an interesting side-bar to the main story.

There were no great financial rewards for Mockridge. In a letter to his father from Nice in August 1955, he wrote that he would receive FF 37,000 for his efforts. By comparison, Gaul was set to receive FF 3 million, which Mockridge estimated was worth £3,000.

"Towards the end of the race we teamed to help him [Gaul] get third place in the general classification, (worth about £1000) and if I am lucky I will get a 10 per cent share of this. But we have no legal agreement."

Mockridge would not become rich through professional cycling, but he had earned international respect and admiration and the personal satisfaction of finishing the toughest and most prestigious cycling race in the world.

The Paris daily *Parisien Libere* wrote that Mockridge had "filled us with admiration."

The Australian had all the disadvantages in the race, yet he stuck it out to finish while other riders – and several famous ones – gave up. We have adopted you, Russell, for good. You have proved yourself as worthy of your glorious predecessor, Hubert Opperman. Next year you will finish among the top ten.

Mockridge had ridden himself into legend. Gaul, the man he had helped into third place, won the Tour de France for Luxembourg in 1958.

Chapter 6

The Rules of the Road

MOCKRIDGE HAD NO difficulty with the unwritten "chop" or "save" arrangements of professional cycling in Australia. Because of the rigours of road racing, it was, and is, impossible to win without an arrangement with others to share the turns of pace during the day and to then share the prize money with those "in for their chop."

It was also known as "the joke" because it is collusion and is, therefore, illegal, and everyone knew about it, but it was unavoidable in road racing. It also operated, more obviously, in track racing and led to public cynicism that track cycling could be rigged.

In sprint racing the winner was generally the rider who had the benefit of protection from team-mates during the race and who could then use his reserves in a dash to the line.

The presence of bookmakers at the two big outdoor track venues in Melbourne – North Essendon and Olympic Park – said there was money to be made.

Generally the contest would be between two stars who would be protected "peas" in a team "pod" and the sprint would determine the winner. Officials were on the lookout and the bookies would be the first to complain if they believed a favourite had performed poorly. But "beating the books" was a badge of honour and cyclists could prearrange the results of races before they were run. All that remained was to signal to a mate in the crowd on a warm-up lap of the local derby who the likely winner would be so the bet could be laid on the long-shot. Those in on the joke would split the profits on the train on the way home.

Mockridge's training mate, Jim Taylor, the constant second to Mockridge in Australia in road racing at the time, put the realities of endurance riding this way:

> We used to split the prize money. We knew that unless we did it that way, we'd both get nothing. We had a bond. We needed each other to win. I rode to win the bike race; he rode to finish it, that was the difference.
>
> We had an opponent's friendship; we were sponsored by different cycling companies [Mockridge rode for Healing, Taylor for Hartley]. He was a vastly superior sprinter. In 1957 I finished second to him eight times.
>
> He had a limit, but it wasn't very often found. There was no one out here who could check him. But we had to help each other. You couldn't ride from Warrnambool to Melbourne without someone sharing the turns of pace. Finishing second meant the same number of pounds in the hand as him.

Max Rowley, who celebrated his and his brother Keith's lives in the 1940s and 1950s in his book *The Rowleys* put their success down to a familial ability to read each other's physical condition, for one to know when to give shelter to the other in the vacuum just off the back wheel, giving the second rider time to recover in the slipstream.

The rule of road racing was that if you were going to ride in the bunch, you did your turn at the front for 100 or 200 metres and then fell back to the tail and let the next rider in the group take the brunt of the wind. Special loathing was reserved for those who took a free ride.

Rowley and his contemporaries were frank about their "saving" or "chop" arrangements, with the qualification that the sprint was the equaliser. They would share the grind through the day, but when it came to the finish, it was "best man wins".

Amateur riders coming into professional racing were often suspicious of "chop" arrangements between seasoned professionals. They could work hard all day doing their turn of pace and then find themselves blocked or out-manoeuvered in a breakaway for the sprint.

Mockridge cited the 1956 Warrnambool to Melbourne race as an example of the shortcomings of the handicap system in Australia, but it's also a commentary on the "chop" in action. In this instance Mockridge was not in on the deal. In fact, he suspected there was a plan to exclude him from the winning stage by leading him out and tiring him. He did not take the bait, held his nerve and set the fastest time.

He set a record for the 262 kilometres and the average time was unmatched anywhere in the world, but he didn't win the race. The handicapper had placed too much lead in the saddlebag. Mockridge's account in *My World on Wheels* is a good description of the unfolding race tactics, which were meant to put him out of contention. It is a good insider description of tactics in a classic Australian road race.

As usual there was no mention of the chop among the scratchmen, who included Peter Panton, Eddie Smith, Peter Anthony, and a surprising addition to the scratch bunch, Sid Patterson. All these riders were riding Malvern Star cycles and were, naturally enough, anxious for a Star victory. Although there was no word to me of any plan to team, it came to me through the ever-present grapevine that there was a chop on and that most of the 11-strong scratch bunch were in it.

I was largely indifferent to plans that had been hatched so early in the race as I was well aware that we would all need each other's help for every mile of the way if we were to have any chance of catching the limit riders who had already been pedalling for more than an hour.

Their arrangement could prove awkward near the finish, however, as they might allow one of their number to breakaway, and refuse to chase him, which would effectively spoil the chances of anyone not in any clandestine carve-up of currency. But Melbourne was a long way off and anything could happen along the way.

An irritant to those in the agreement was that if I should win, I would not have to share with them – and on form they knew that I had the strongest finishing sprint.

The first incident along the way was after we had covered only 10 miles [16 kilometres]. Sid Patterson dropped off the back of the fast-moving bunch. He had had enough for the day and retired to the comfort of his sedan. Next to be unhooked was Peter Panton, the Western Australian. He left us a few miles after Sid retired.

The remainder of the bunch stayed together and worked as I have never known a bunch to work, before or since. Every man's turn of pace was truly phenomenal and it seemed like a snappy, out of breath five-miler, instead of the longest one-day race in Australia. Through Panmure, Garvoc, Terang, Camperdown and Weerite we raced, along roads lined with spectators – almost as many as you would see in France.

What a pace! Up to the front of the bunch, 15 hard pumps on the pedals, swing to the side, let the rider on your rear wheel take over the job of pacing, catch up with your deficiency of oxygen as you wait for the last man in the Indian file to pass, tack on to the back, hold your front tyre as near as possible to the spinning rear wheel of the man in front until you get a buffeting from the wind, and then you know you are the leader again...another hard turn of pace, and so it goes on, mile after mile.

This is team work. Each doing his spell of the chase at the head of the line, streamlined over his machine, eyes scrutinising the road ahead for anything that might puncture a tyre and spoil any chance of success.

As we raced through Geelong, I saw that the crowds in my hometown were 20 deep by the roadside. They were all yelling encouragement to the local boy. I hoped that I would not let them down. By this time we had picked up riders dropped from other bunches, and sometimes we engulfed complete groups. The greater our numbers grew, the slower and less efficient our turns of pace became. Our machine-like workmanship of a few miles back was gone and we were now just an over-large amorphous posse of pedallers. Sometimes the pace would speed up to 27–28mph [43–45km/h], other times it became a mere plod. Reason for this was that the size of the group made it impossible to keep the riders we had collected along the way out of our paths. They were hampering us, mostly unintentionally, from keeping our former pace. The sympathy of any rider on a mark will always be with fellow middle and limit markers and not with the scratchmen. I remember saying to one rider who had got tangled up with our bunch and was being a terrible nuisance merely be getting in our way "Get out of the way can't you?"

He replied "You don't think I'm here to help you blokes, do you?"

We were about 50 strong at Werribee, 19 miles [30 kilometres] from the finish and the bunch had become so unwieldy that it was impossible to ride to any system. It became apparent that we would not catch the few remaining riders ahead of us.

It was just past this town that I saw a little of how the chop in the scratch bunch was to operate. I was about 10 from the front at the time. One of the riders opened up a gap on the bunch, and went off in a solo bid either to catch the limit men or gain the fastest time award.

The remainder of the scratch combination immediately stopped their strong turns of pace. The chop was in action. The intention was obvious. While the rider was off on his own, the others would leave it to me, and anyone else who might feel inclined, to chase him. I could easily have pursued and caught him, at this time his lead was slender; but I knew that once caught, he too would stop riding hard; the others would then set off after us at full bore and we would be caught easily. The effort of chasing him would have used up some of the energy that I would need for the final sprint.

The cabal might have had an alternative scheme in mind. This would be that I would give chase, catch him, and then be allowed to keep a lead of, say, half a mile ahead of the field. This is known as dangling a rider, the same as an angler plays with a fish. He will let it tire itself out at the end of his line, and then when the fish is tired, the angler leisurely pulls him in.

I was not in the mood to play games with them, and to the visible distraction of some, I held my place in the bunch and awaited developments. It was then a war of nerves. My hunch was the breakaway would tire and be retrieved by the main platoon. This was what I was hoping for, but for a while it looked like I would be disappointed. His pace increased and his lead became almost half a mile, and then three-quarters of a mile.

The others in the joke pedalled in leisurely fashion, and eyed me as if to say "Well aren't you going to chase him? You'd better hurry up if you are!" His figure became smaller and smaller and smaller on the wide strip of highway, and was about to disappear out of sight when it suddenly became larger and larger. Gradually we overtook him. We felt a wind whipping in our faces and the reason for his weakening became apparent. His gamble had failed because the wind had changed direction.

The scratch bunch entered the Melbourne Showground with Mockridge in a commanding position and no deal in place. The £80 for fastest time would not be shared.

He won the race in the record time of 5 hours 47 minutes 5 seconds. Mockridge had taken 18 minutes off a record set by Eddie Smith the year before. The time stood as a record for 24 years. He rode at an average speed of 44.2 km/h.

Mockridge and the scratch bunch finished faster over the distance than any group of riders in the world – the previous record for the same distance was the Paris–Tours race of 1955, won by Jacques Dupont in 5 hours 47 minutes and 48 seconds – yet the scratch bunch had failed to catch the limit riders and the glory of line honours, a failure that Mockridge put down to the "iniquity" of the handicap system.

Hec Sutherland was second to me in the sprint. His father was waiting for him at the trackside and after a slow-down lap, Hec pedalled over to him and asked "what was that worth Dad" meaning how much was the prize for second-fastest time. Mr Sutherland accurately and tersely replied "nothing". Hec had ridden 163 miles for just that. He did receive a case of well-known soft drink, as did the first 40 riders to finish. Hardly adequate compensense [sic] for a tough day's work.

The following year, 1957, he rode from scratch with Jim Taylor and again won fastest time. John Burrowes recalled:

> The task defeated 11 of the nation's fittest in 1956; in 1957 the task was allotted three men. As it turned out Eddie Smith failed to start and Russell and Jim Taylor formed the smallest scratch group in the classic's history. Ahead of them lay the toughest task in the race's records.
>
> But even Smith's withdrawal meant no difference to the handicap. Few gave them a hope of achieving anything in the race.
>
> But six hours, six minutes later at the Showgrounds track, Russell sprinted ahead of Taylor to be the fastest man to cover the distance. They had done the impossible. The time was only two minutes slower than Smith's record of 1955, when the scratch bunch was 17 strong, and 19 minutes slower than Russell's own record in 1956. The pair had averaged 27 mph for the 163 miles [43km/h for 262 kilometres], which is one of the most remarkable performances ever recorded by two roadmen.

Burrowes recorded Taylor saying it was the greatest suffering he had ever known and for many miles he had been merely clinging to Mockidge's wheel.

Jim Taylor said the two spoke only three or four times in the ride, so focused were they on the pursuit of the riders in front of them.

The pair was moving so fast that none of the second scratch group riders could join them as they were passed. Mockridge did not know this and when Taylor came past to do a turn of pace, he asked, "Where's second scratch" – expecting the new group to join them. Taylor replied, "We've passed them."

> Coming through Winchelsea and I'd had a flat spot and was going to give it away and he told me to "keep it going" and the same thing happened to him just before Werribee.
> Up the Belmont Hill in Geelong in top gear...we had the 10-minute group in sight coming into Geelong and I thought we were going to catch them, but they took the bit and we didn't, but we went through Geelong at a great rate of knots, and we rattled a bit on the way to Werribee, from about Lara things got pretty tough and Russell said "looks like we've had it" but he did not slacken speed and kept up the pursuit...

Mockridge described the conundrum this way:

> Whether it's a "joke", "chop" or "save", it does not necessarily mean a fixed race. In fact, because of the pre-race arrangements, the public is often treated to a much more entertaining spectacle, and professional racing is, after all, as much an entertainment as it is a sport.
> If there were no plans before each race, there would be very little chance of the scratch men or backmarkers retrieving the limit riders, who are given as much as 200 yards start in a one-mile race. These arrangements are illegal of course, but officialdom is merely burying its head in the sand, ostrich fashion, if they endeavour to pretend that they do not exist.

According to Harry Gordon, Mockridge was a victim of collusion by other riders.

Usually he refused to enter into schemes aimed at pooling the prize money, and he rode all-out to win every event. His reputation was resented by some riders, and often it was obvious that a squad of cyclists had ganged up in a "chop" arrangement to squeeze him out.

It would be ludicrous to suggest though, that Mockridge was never party to arrangements. He was a realist, and he knew that it was often necessary, particularly as a scratch-marker, to share the pacing with another cyclist. On the comparatively rare occasions when he did arrange to share prize money with others, it was usually done during a race and mostly as a defence against the teaming of other riders.

Mockridge had a saying, "Before you can learn to win a race you have to learn to finish it."

Mockridge backed his extraordinary physical ability with a steely individualism and self-sufficiency that set him apart from the pack.

Chapter 7

The Five-Ring Circus

MOCKRIDGE KEENLY OBSERVED the hypocrisy and inconsistencies in the division between amateur and professional sport, which his stand against the Olympic bond had brought attention to.

Arriving back in Australia after winning two gold medals in Helsinki, he turned up at the North Essendon board track, where a welcome home extravaganza, complete with fireworks in the form of the five-ringed Olympic symbol, was underway.

The promoters were making a killing off a record, fee-paying crowd.

Amateurs were not supposed to accept any monetary reward for their success. These were the rules that had decided the fate of many sportsmen. Juniors who had taken a pound in prize money at club events were forever excluded from the highest echelon of their sport because they had sullied the privileged notion of the Olympic ideal.

And if the Australian Olympic Federation paid the fare to Helsinki or London, it did not want its athletes cashing in on their Olympic success through advertising or sponsorship contracts with bike retailers.

So as Russell Mockridge and Lionel Cox stood on a dais at

Russell Mockridge Souvenir Card, produced by Healing Cycles 1958.
Reproduced with permission of the Mockridge family.

Cover of *The Australian Cyclist*, June 1949.

Mockridge beats John Tresidder to the line at Hurstville Oval, Sydney, 1951.

Mockridge and Lionel Cox in tandem.

Mockridge and his new wife Irene at their wedding in Sydenham, South London, September 1953.

Mockridge with his mother, Claire, and his father, Bob, after the Helsinki Olympics.

Medallists of the Helsinki 2,000-metre tandem race. From left: South Africans Raymond Robinson and Thomas Shardelow, Australians Lionel Cox and Russell Mockridge and Italians Antonio Maspes and Cesare Pinarello.

Mockridge's triumphant homecoming to Geelong after winning two gold medals in Helsinki, 1952.

Mockridge borrowed a bicycle from Jack Baker to collect his own equipment after returning to Geelong following the Helsinki Olympic Games.

Reproduced with permission of the *Herald and Weekly Times* Photographic Collection.

Mockridge with his trainer and mechanic, Les Dunne, at the Bendigo Cycling Carnival.

Russell Mockridge with manager, Gino Bambagiotti.

the North Essendon board track, listening to local dignitaries remind them that they were "very lucky boys" to have been given the opportunity to represent their country, and watching the Olympic-themed fireworks, Mockridge pondered on a system that could reward cycling promoters, yet denied "any possibility of a cyclist making any money out of whatever he may have gained for himself, after years of hard training and much out of pocket expenses."

Mockridge's views on the double standards in the sport had hardened in 1952, when he came to understand that before he could be included in the Olympic team for Helsinki he had to sign an agreement to remain an amateur for two years after the Games. Default on the agreement incurred a £750 penalty. Mockridge had decided to turn professional after the Helsinki Games, putting himself at the intersection of Olympic idealism, economic pragmatism and his conscience.

He'd made up his mind to return to Europe in 1952. He was happy to start his Continental tour with the Helsinki Games, but not at the expense of "mortgaging two years of my cycling life." He would pay his own fare to Europe. He declared he would not sign the Olympic bond.

This was a matter of conscience as far as he was concerned. But others concerned that Australia's chances of winning medals would be limited without Mockridge. He was setting world-standard track times and, in February 1952, at the Australian championships in Adelaide, won the 1,000-metre sprint, 1,000-metre time trial, one mile (1.6 kilometres), five mile (eight kilometres), and with Hec Sutherland, the tandem titles.

There was plenty of advice to sign the bond and deal with the consequences later, but this, in his view, would be dishonest, since he had made his plans to turn professional straight after the Games. He wrote:

> I suppose I could have just signed the bond and left it to them to force the issue when I eventually turned professional, but I considered that this would have been morally wrong. I had every intention of turning professional and I was almost certain that it would be well within the stipulated two-year period. With this knowledge I could not sign the bond in good faith.

The stand-off came to a head after lobbying from Hubert Opperman, *The Sporting Globe* and Geelong dignitaries. On the eve of the Games, and based in London for his European campaign, Mockridge agreed to sign a one-year bond.

He arrived in Helsinki after the Games had begun and was partnered with Lionel Cox, a down-to-earth Sydney sprinter whose strength was built on hard labour at the Sydney fruit and vegetable markets. The two complemented and supported each other and both had a successful Games.

His modesty and his view of the value of Olympic success combined to find expression in the two pages Mockridge gave to winning two gold medals at Helsinki. Entire books have been based on a single gold medal. Mockridge won two in one day becoming the first Australian cyclist to achieve dual gold at the same Olympics.

Mockridge wrote 212 pages in his autobiography. He devoted only 1 per cent of it to the extraordinary effort of winning the 1,000-metre time trial on the morning of July 31, 1958, setting a world record, and then without mechanic, trainer or coach, riding the tandem sprint to take gold with Lionel Cox on the back.

But in his head he had turned professional and the Olympic gold did not glisten for him.

Lionel Cox also put in a big day. After winning gold with Mockridge on the tandem he took on the world amateur champion Enzo Sacchi in the 1,000 metre sprint, losing by half a wheel.

Mockridge had ridden into Australian Olympic history, becoming Australia's first dual cycling gold medallist.

The hard-line demarcation between amateur and professional was a sore point for athletes, particularly cyclists and runners, who had to choose between an idealised "pure" world of amateur sport with its gilded Olympic crown, or the world of professional sport, where athletes made money from prizes, sponsors, advertisers and promoters.

But there was no pot of gold. Most professional athletes struggled to cover their expenses. But in the eyes of hard-liners in the Olympic movement, they had abandoned high ideals and sold out for the filthy lucre.

This dual-track system was vigorously endorsed by the amateur officials who seemed to take great delight in scouring the sports results of local clubs, compiling blacklists of young riders who had accepted a cash prize.

Jim Taylor's fate was decided early in his life when he accepted a £1 prize at a Stratford cycle club event.

Riders such as Keith and Max Rowley hardly noticed an amateur division. Professional events were held all over country and metropolitan Victoria. If you were good enough, you raced as a professional and tried to cover your travel and expenses. If you won, it was your shout.

Mockridge's protest put the spotlight on the noddyland inhabited by well-meaning Olympic officials. The high-minded ideals of the Olympic movement did not translate into practice for athletes. By the 1980s, reality had checked the Olympic ideal and professionals were allowed into the Olympic circle. In 2008, Australian rider Cadel Evans rode into second place in the Tour de France in July and then immediately began preparing for the road event at the Beijing Olympics.

The wheel had turned.

Chapter 8

The Rival

IF MOCKRIDGE WORE the white hat then his opponent in the black was Sid Patterson.

Patterson was cheese to Mockridge's chalk. They came from different backgrounds – Patterson was Irish Catholic, playful and outgoing. He was a post-war pin-up boy.

Mockridge had described himself as intellectual and diffident. His rivals added the colour with names such as China Doll, a reference to fragility, and Little Lord Fauntleroy, a reference to his natty dress style. And he was WASP – White, Anglo-Saxon, Protestant.

The promoters accentuated their differences and the rivalry between the two camps was intense.

Herald-Sun journalist Ron Reed remembered Patto as a larger-than-life personality who was a force and a face behind the scenes in the *Sun* Tour long after he had retired. He enjoyed the camaraderie and the atmosphere of the Tour. In his day athletes drank and smoked, and then got up the next morning and rode through their hangover with the aid of a bacon and egg sandwich, a cup of tea and a couple of Bex powders.

Reed, writing after Patterson's death, captured him as a "showman and a larrikin, an ebullient, happy-go-lucky character who loved nothing more than a beer and a laugh with people he liked – in other words the sort of bloke whose friendship was highly regarded by everybody who ever earned it."

Reed remembered his "astonishing capacity to enjoy himself to all hours and still get on the bike after a few hours sleep and destroy the world's best riders."

Patto – the Ox was his nickname – was a formidable track rider and a respectable road rider too. He was stocky and strong and could deliver in the sprint, but he never matched it on the road with Mockridge, blaming the forces of gravity for his poor performances in road racing.

He won four world championship sprint events among 300 professional titles before retiring in 1968. Patto died in 1999, aged 72, after a battle with cancer.

He and Mockridge rode very successfully together as a six-day team in Paris in the first half of 1955. Six-day races were another version of non-stop endurance events that were popular in pre-television Europe and Britain. A team of three had to have a member on the indoor track at all times. Time trials and sprints were called randomly and teams earned points over the six days. It echoed of the dance marathons of Depression-era America.

Patterson's home ground was the North Essendon and Olympic Park velodromes, outdoor tracks on shaky timber frames that operated between November and April and packed in noisy mobs, bookmakers and beer and hot dog vendors on Saturday nights.

The atmosphere was heightened by the noise of the boards, which rattled as the riders raced over them. The North Essendon track closed around 1958. The Olympic Park track was demolished in 1972.

The boards at North Essendon were freshly painted each summer and fine sand spread over the white paint before it dried to increase traction.

The "walls of death" angles on the two turns were 50 degrees. North Essendon was a relatively short circuit at 231 metres, which made for fast laps and a corny commentary of "thrills and spills" and "gravity-defying" riding.

Max Rowley captured the atmosphere and the attitudes when he related his strategy for winning the "secret distance" event which often wrapped up a Saturday night's racing at the Essendon track.

The cyclists would only know that the race was to finish when an official held up a flag indicating a two-lap sprint home. If you were not in a forward position when the finish was called, it would be difficult to win. But Max had figured out how to beat the system.

"I always backed my theory that the race had to finish five minutes before the last train was to leave the North Essendon [now Strathmore] railway station at 10.45pm."

Max would work out the time allocated to the race on the basis that the program always finished at 10.40pm.

"If we were ready to start at 10.28pm, then the race would be 12 minutes or a little over five miles. If we were to start at 10.32pm, then the eight minutes would allow about 25 laps."

This was family entertainment pre-television and was staged by promoters with one foot firmly planted in side-show alley.

Six-day races, pacing behind motor bikes, even pacing behind trains on specially laid tracks to set records, were all part of the gimmicky stunts promoters used to get publicity.

There were records claimed for all sorts of extraordinary

feats: non-stop rides from Sydney to Melbourne; rides across the Nullabor Plain; rides around Australia; anything that would get attention and a local or metropolitan headline.

The integrity of claims for these endurance records was sometimes suspect. Who was to know if the rider was pedalling stoically towards another endurance record or fast asleep in the caravan, while a substitute took over, in the consuming darkness of a country road.

Even the revered Hubert Opperman had to put up with accusations of fixing. Journalist Neil Kearney recalls a story of a flush-faced Sid Patterson taking a bit of skin off the cyclist-turned-Federal Member for Corio by heckling from the back of a meeting, "Tell them about the piano wire Oppy," a reference to rumours that promoter and manager Bruce Small had towed the great man, secretly, at least some of the way, across the Nullabor Plain to claim his 1930s record of 13.5 days to cover 4,427 kilometres from Freemantle to Sydney.

And you won't see anything like the Hartley window display again.

Max and Keith Rowley, contracted to Hartley Cycles, were regular exhibits in the bike shop's Flinders Street store windows in 1949. Flinders Street pedestrian traffic was brought to a halt as people stopped and took in the spectacle.

> Keith would be talking about assembling a cycle while I pedalled away on the rollers. Then he would start talking about a particular road race that I had been successful in the previous year. It had only been two years since we moved from the three-speed gears to a multiple of eight gears using a double chain wheel. With eight gears it was easy to simulate just what happened in a race. I was able to exaggerate speed changes by increasing or decreasing the revolutions of my

pedals to fit with Keith's interpretation of the event – whether we had a tailwind, headwind, downhill or uphill.

Then of course every race included what we call a jam – a time when a very fast pace is set in an attempt to get away from the other riders. The climax of every race presentation was naturally a frantic finishing sprint. Keith would then ride the rollers whilst I had the talking part. This all helped to publicise big cycling road races and, of course, ourselves, as well as our sponsors, Hartleys.

World of Sport, the live Channel 7 Sunday morning sports show, was the last local incarnation of cycling and circus. Patto performed on the rollers for as long as he could, Brylcreemed, well-groomed and well-supported by sporting peers Lou Richards, Jack Dyer and Ron Casey. Patto and the football heroes of the day were entrées to the traditional Sunday lamb roast that celebrated a clear day off work.

Mockridge said that European stars coming out to Australia in the 1950s to ride the board tracks mistakenly thought they were here for a holiday.

Riding five nights a week, the top riders would be expected to ride a three-heat match race, heat and final of a derby, heat and, if successful, final of a mile handicap, and finally a five-mile scratch race.

The rivalry with Patterson came to a head in the 1957 track season and the prestigious Austral Wheel Race.

Mockridge was clearly unhappy with the pre-race negotiations, instigated by the Patterson camp, over how the race should be run.

The problem for Mockridge was that his two fellow scratch riders, Patterson and Oscar Plattner, rode for Malvern Star, while he rode for Healing.

Mockridge inferred that the Patterson camp was prepared to pay him to lose – for an eighth share of the prize money. He would ride a gallant finish and share his prize money with a rider who would "take" Mockridge, in his slipstream, to a credible finish.

This was untenable to Mockridge because the proposal had him, and his bike company sponsor, losing to his principal rival.

Mockridge initially saw the problem as the third man or two-against-one dilemma.

He had faced the problem in Europe against Enzo Sacchi and Marino Morettini in 1951, and against Jan Derksen and Reg Harris in the 1952 Paris Open Grand Prix.

He knew that a three-man sprint race would be difficult to win even if all three backmarkers were cooperating.

The odds were that Plattner would give Patterson a ride home in the last couple of laps, giving the laurels to Patterson and Malvern Star. As Mockridge wrote:

> Each year we hear the old cry: Why can't the scratch men all work equal turns of pace and the best man wins at the finish? The people who voice this theory are idealists or they do not themselves believe what they say. The tremendous prestige and publicity that a scratch man would gain from an Austral win completely eliminates any possibility of any scratch man working absolutely flat out throughout the race. The chance that your fellow scratch man is holding back a just a little for the final sprint is just too great.

Mockridge was concerned for his prestige and the name of his sponsor if he lost to Patterson. He was not going to play the role of *domestique*, or worker, and see Patterson and Plattner take the glory and the prize money.

The offer of an inducement seems to have come late in the piece, after he had turned down the idea of cooperating with Patterson and Plattner because he feared his run home would be blocked in the closing stages of the race.

> It was put to me that I ought to assist in "taking" one of my fellow riders in the final for an eighth share of the prize money. I refused point-blank and kept on refusing to enter into any sort of "arrangement" for the final. The overtures went on right up to the line-up on the Saturday night as the 14 finalists were staggered around the track, ready to chase the big money, before a capacity crowd.

There was no deal and the race was won by a frontmarker. In Mockridge's mind it was better to lose to a frontmarker than be beaten by Patterson.

The running of the 1958 Austral was left to John Burrowes to tell. That year Mockridge had a pre-race discussion with Patterson, Barry Waddell and Keith Reynolds. The four would join forces to catch the frontmarkers. Reynolds and Waddell would sacrifice their own chances of winning in the sprint by doing the bulk of the chasing. This would leave Patterson and Mockridge to fight it out on a "best man wins" basis.

It was not to be. In the final lap, as Mockridge and Patterson closed in on the frontmarkers, Mockridge and a rider named Kevin Latter came too close. There was an audible twang as Latter's pedal hit Mockridge's wheel.

Out of the confusion came a charge of five riders thrusting at the finish line.

The winner was New Zealander Neil Geraghty. Second was Kevin McKenzie. Third was Mockridge. Patterson was fourth.

Mockridge wrote that a local reporter once asked Sid Patterson for some details of his training program.

Sid told him, "I don't get time to train – I'm too busy racing."

Ron Reed related a classic Patterson tale in his tribute to Patto in the *Herald-Sun* after this death.

> One of his cohorts was the late, great E.J. Whitten, one of the few men who could match him glass for glass. On one of their last circuits together they got thirsty even earlier than usual – just after breakfast in fact – and knocked on the door of a country pub.
>
> The publican eventually answered it in his pyjamas and informed them that he did not open until 11am. 'You do now', they said in unison – and he did.

In my mind's eye I see a bloke wearing a hat in the 1950s narrow-brimmed style, walking away from the Olympic Park board track at the end of Saturday night, wheeling a bike, a gladstone bag in the other hand, heading home, the job done for another week.

Chapter 9

July 31, 1952:
A Golden Day

RUSSELL MOCKRIDGE ARRIVED in Helsinki four days before he was scheduled to compete.

There'd been months of argy-bargy between Mockridge and Olympic officials over his refusal to sign a "fidelity bond" which obliged him to stay amateur for two years after the Olympics.

Four months before the Games were to begin, Mockridge left by boat to compete against Europe's best cyclists, adamant he would not sign, and he was subsequently dropped from the team.

But he was very successful. In the first half of 1952, he beat the amateur world champion Enzo Sacchi three times. On July 6 he won the prestigious amateur Paris Grand Prix sprint race, which qualified him to compete in the Open Grand Prix the next day.

This was the real race, the professionals' race. The amateur winner was not expected to win. Professional reputations and contracts were at stake.

But win he did, in powerful fashion.

He won his heat and went into a semi-final with the reigning world champion Reg Harris (England), which Harris won after Mockridge led all the way.

Mockridge then went into a *repechage* or second life event against Dutch rider Arie Van Vliet, Sid Patterson and Frenchman Jacques Bellenger.

Patterson and Bellenger were locked in a tactical duel, which allowed Van Vliet and Mockridge to get ahead.

His lone-wolf instincts took over again and he took another "flier" 400 metres from the finish. This time it paid off and he was in the final against Jan Derksen and Reg Harris.

The final would be a classic battle of nerves. Mockridge was determined to win the tactical battle and not be the first rider to lead out. Instead of setting the pace, he wanted to be in the rear. He also knew the two professionals would team against him if he gave them the chance. So the three of them balanced on their machines for six minutes after the start of the race. Mockridge, the amateur, was expected to break but didn't; Derksen went first, with Harris on his wheel, but after 50 metres they stopped again. This time for five minutes. As Mockridge wrote:

> Again it was Derksen to make the first move and again it was Harris to go with him. That suited me fine. Derksen wound the pace up fairly slowly until nearing the furlong when we were almost at top speed. By the furlong we were all sprinting very hard but I was still in my favourite box seat. Derksen then gave way to Harris, who made a direct dash for the line. My plan then was to try and pass him midway on the straight. This I found I could do fairly easily, and the result appeared to have quite an effect on Reg. I can remember glimpsing his look of surprise as I passed.

Mockridge's win intensified pressure on Olympic officials to back down and put Mockridge in the team for the very good reason that the "champion from the Antipodes" could win gold medals for Australia.

The breakthrough came after Jim Blake, a reporter on the Melbourne *Sporting Globe*, telephoned the mayor of Geelong, Cr Bevan Purnell, suggesting that Mockridge's hometown should put up the bond.

Purnell offered to guarantee the £750 for the bond if the Australian Olympic Federation would shorten the term to one year. AOF officials agreed to this compromise and Purnell telephoned Mockridge in London and he agreed to the deal.

The *Sporting Globe* and the mayor of Geelong had succeeded where politicians, including the influential Hubert Opperman, had failed. The bond scheme was eventually scrapped, thanks to Mockridge.

There to greet Mockridge in Helsinki was a pack of Australian newspapermen, including Harry Gordon, covering his first Olympic Games.

The fact that Mockridge had agreed to compete was front page news. Mockridge had changed his mind and signed the bond. He was beating the best in Europe. He was a gold medal hope for Australia. But the champion was more focused on finding out where he was sleeping than answering reporters' questions at 2am that midsummer day.

What happened four days after his arrival is cycling history. On a wind-swept track at the Helsinki Velodrome, Mockridge won the 1,000-metres time trial in Olympic record time of 1 minute.11.1 seconds. That same afternoon, although he normally rested for three days after a strenuous time trial, he partnered Lionel Cox to win the tandem title. Inside a couple of hours he and Cox – who gained a silver medal in the sprint – had given Australia the most successful Olympic day she had ever had.

But, more important to Mockridge, he had squared matters with the people of his hometown, Geelong, whose efforts enabled him to join the Games team at virtually the last minute.

Gordon later revisited the AOF decision on the Mockridge case in his 1994 book *Australia and the Olympic Games*. Mockridge probably never understood how lucky he was to be cleared for competition.

It was, in fact, a decision that went to the wire. The casting vote belonged to executive member Bill Uren, who was to show unusually good political judgement.

Mockridge was initially named in the AOF's first team of 35 for Helsinki and given until April 15, 1952 to sign. A few days before the deadline, Mockridge sent the secretary of the AOF, Edgar Tanner a telegram: "REGRET UNWILLING TO SIGN BOND FULL STOP REGARDS RUSSELL MOCKRIDGE."

He was dropped. In the meantime, Mockridge was enjoying a purple patch in Europe while his supporters, including Opperman, beat the drum for him in Australia. Edgar Tanner was strongly opposed to varying the bond. Bill Uren believed accommodating Mockridge would set a bad example and diminish the AOF's reputation.

Tanner and Uren, who was also the Australian team manager, met Mockridge in London after he had won the Paris grands prix in early July, but there was no agreement.

Once the one-year bond idea was floated, the AOF chairman, Harry Alderson, decided to put the matter to a vote. According to Gordon, Alderson let it be known that he was happy with the proposal. One by one the five executive members said their piece.

Executive member Hugh Weir was against any reduction of the bond term, but Rex Wallman, South Australia's representative, backed Alderson.

Then Edgar Tanner spoke and he was as hard line as ever: "The other team members have to sign for two years, and anyway I'm opposed to having the AOF do anything to assist a man to turn professional." It was two-all. Uren would decide the issue.

Uren decided to back the chairman rather than humiliate him and bring the AOF into further disrepute. He later wrote: "Had there been a round-table discussion by the executive, I would have advocated a full-term bond...but since the chairman had made public statements approving of the procedure, I considered the interests of the Federation and the national prestige would be best served by the inclusion of Mockridge in the team."

Uren made the right call. The days of the bond were numbered.

Chapter 10

Percy Cerutty

RUSSELL MOCKRIDGE MET the flamboyant athletics coach Percy Cerutty on the voyage back to Australia after the Helsinki Games. Mockridge was suddenly famous. Cerutty's athletes had performed below expectation, but he wasn't showing any remorse, according to biographer Graem Sims in his 2003 study of Cerutty, *Why Die?*

John Landy had failed to qualify in either the 1,500-metre or 5,000-metre events; Les Perry finished sixth in the 5,000 metres against Emil Zatopek; and Don Macmillan finished 9th in the 1,500 metres, the metric mile.

Don Macmillan had the biggest grievance against his coach, though they were all unhappy with his publicity-seeking style.

The night before the 1,500-metre final, the sports medicine researcher Professor Frank Cotton visited Macmillan and Cerutty at the Olympic Village and started discussing warm up preparations.

The outcome was that Macmillan and Cerutty agreed to a dehydrating warm up regime that had Macmillan jogging, dressed in two track suits, with a towel wrapped around his head, just hours before the race.

When he went onto the track he was exhausted and dehydrated. He couldn't even speak. Macmillan still managed to run his best time and finished 9th.

Cerutty berated the sports scientist for using his runner as a guinea pig, but Cerutty was the coach and had allowed it to happen. But there was no apology from Cerutty. The athletes at Helsinki had seen how other coaches worked; how they discussed tactics and strategy before races. Cerutty was strong on preparation and strength building, but there was no science to his theories. He had theories about fitness and training regimes that were ahead of their time and he marketed himself forcefully. But he was unpredictable and erratic and sometimes a negative influence on race days because of his attention-seeking behaviour.

The Australian cycling team had no section manager or mechanic, never mind a coach, and Mockridge was intrigued by the rambunctious Cerutty, though his runners were medalless at Helsinki.

Australia had claimed six gold medals: one to breaststroker John Davies, two to 100-metre and 200-metre sprinter Marjorie Jackson, one to Shirley Strickland and two to Russell Mockridge (one shared with Lionel Cox).

According to Sims, who had access to Cerutty's papers, the coach described Russell Mockridge as the most extraordinary athlete he had ever met. The two became close friends, sharing ideas on fitness, diet, philosophy and religion.

Together with Melbourne wrestler Kevin Coote, Mockridge and Cerutty ran a competitive eight-kilometre course around the deck of the ship each morning ahead of a day of relaxation and socialising.

Sims wrote that the two hit it off immediately, "Percy's

flamboyance complementing Mockridge's introspection and melancholia."

> With ample time on the boat for discourse, Percy was able to delve into the Mockridge persona, uncover his theology, and discover a man with similar drives to his own, exploring the transformational possibilities of supreme effort.

Mockridge wrote of how Cerutty, a runner in his youth, had given sport away in his twenties and by his thirties was in poor health, suffering from migraine headaches and stomach disorders. Doctors were offering no solutions.

> He was over 40 when he first became aware of health food – wholemeal bread, raw vegetables, fruit and the like. Willing to try anything, he took to a diet which was as natural as possible. The results were as amazing as they were speedy. Almost overnight Percy's ailments vanished, and he became a complete convert, not only to the food of nature, but to a simpler way of life, with plenty of exercise, and anything that could be classified as clean, healthy and natural existence.

Percy Cerutty gave Mockridge confidence to pursue an individual lifestyle and philosophy. Cerutty endorsed the idea of physical perfection as being worthy in itself. Percy added the philosophy of Plato and the Stoics to the physical hardness of the Spartans and came up with Stotanism to describe his alternative philosophy. In the pursuit of physical perfection Mockridge found essential truths and seemed at his happiest.

By 1954 Cerutty had met Nancy Armstrong and the two made plans to develop his bush block at Portsea on the

Mornington Peninsula in Victoria into a training camp for promising athletes.

"Marry me," said Cerutty to Nancy, "and you will never have to cook again," in a reference to his belief in whole foods.

Conditions were primitive, but that was part of the appeal to Cerutty and the small group of friends and athletes who visited and enjoyed the physical training, the natural beauty of the Bass Strait beaches, the wholesome food and the company of like-minded souls.

Mockridge came back into Cerutty's life in 1956, when he and Irene returned to Australia after their three years in Europe.

Russell and Irene soon became regular weekend visitors. Cerutty's first group of promising athletes – John Landy, Don Macmillan and Les Perry – were now estranged from the "seer of the sandhills", and Herb Elliot, who would restore Cerutty's reputation as an athletics coach at the Commonwealth Games at Cardiff in 1958 and Rome in 1960, was not yet in the camp.

Visitors included Warragul marathon runner Geoff Watt, whose daughter, Kathy, would become Australia's first female cyclist to win a gold medal for the individual road race at Barcelona in 1992.

The visitors would run around the Portsea golf course and the Hall circuit, a track just over a mile long, through the scrub around the back beach road that became a Portsea training camp institution.

Another test was the Sandhill, the steepest dune between the camp and the back beach. Mockridge established a record for the ascent of the Sandhill – 11 seconds up the 24.4 metre dune at an angle of 45 degrees – that would never be bettered in the history of the training camp by any athlete from any discipline.

Cerutty was in Sweden when news broke of Mockridge's death in September 1958. Russell, Irene and Lindy were to visit Cerutty and Nancy at Portsea the following weekend. Cerutty rattled off a lengthy tribute to his friend in a heroic style.

> I knew Russell well, and to this I attest –
> Of all the men known to me, Russell was best!
> I rally: I strengthen: to live to this thought.
> Humanity, surely, that never was bought.
> By motive: by deed: for no action was base:
> If ever a man shall see Christ face to face!
> Maybe, and I feel it is true – Yes 'tis true!
> My friend Russell Mockridge was one of the few,
> A lesson: example: for all in part can –
> Learn to live, as liv'd Russell, complete as a man!

Cerutty told Harry Gordon that winning actually bored Russell Mockridge.

> He couldn't be bothered winning...I suppose you could say he lacked the killer spirit. He felt he was capable of something more brilliant. In 1955 he told me he wanted to take on professional running. He was one of the best natural sprinters I ever saw, and he used to run for hours over the sand at Portsea. We were going to set him for the Stawell Gift, but he lost interest. He was a sensitive, tormented sort of fellow...the most unusual athlete I ever met.

Chapter 11

Lionel Cox

RUSSELL MOCKRIDGE FOUND friendship and support in Lionel Cox, the nuggety Sydney fruit market labourer who he teamed up with at the Helsinki Olympics. They were from different backgrounds but they complemented each other. Newtown-born Cox was a tough and aggressive sprinter, but had an easy-going personality and was handy with equipment. Mockridge, the fast-ascending track rider from Melbourne, had seniority and had Cox's respect. They were both in top form and they clicked.

Mockridge treated Cox with great decency, though at the expense of his own fortunes, and let him keep his spot in the 1,000-metre sprint event at Helsinki. The spot had gone to Cox because of Mockridge's indecision. Arriving at Helsinki after the Games had started, Mockridge could have bumped Cox and taken the ride against the reigning amateur world champion Enzo Sacchi.

This would have been a dramatic contest. Mockridge and Sacchi were very evenly matched in European racing and there was tension between them.

In 1951, Mockridge lost the world amateur sprint championships in Milan to Sacchi in a three-man final where

Sacchi's partner, Marino Morettini, played a spoiling role, leading Mockridge out and setting Sacchi up for the win.

A week later, Mockridge and Sacchi met in a two-man match race in Turin, which Mockridge won easily.

In the run up to the Games of 1952 Mockridge beat Sacchi in the Amateur Grand Prix de Paris. With Mockridge clear to compete at Helsinki, a showdown between the world's two best amateur sprinters was now on the horizon.

This was a promoter's dream, and a gold medal chance for Mockridge and Australia.

But Mockridge took the less glamorous time trial event. He would race against the clock. Cox would race Sacchi. The rider to beat in the time trial would be Marino Morettini.

Cox repaid the gesture by taking charge of the tandem bike that Mockridge had brought from London, but which was in parts and had to be assembled. There was no mechanic, there was not even a liaison officer between the Australian cyclists and the Australian team managers. Cox recalled:

> We'd never ridden one. We just put it together, had a try out and away we went.
>
> We went there as individual bike riders and all of a sudden bingo, Russell's going to ride the time trial. He decided I would ride the sprint, and all of a sudden up comes this tandem. I'd never even ridden one before.
>
> We made up our own bloody mind to ride it. There were hardly any officials there, or any jurisdiction for us, we just put it together and that was it.
>
> In 1952 we didn't expect any tandem. We got the tandem given to us. Someone in London getting on the plane gave the tandem to Mockridge. "Here take this, you might use it." That was how it eventuated. It was a last minute affair and we put our things together and that was it.

We rode, we enjoyed what we were doing and we were very happy with the result.

We were both going exceptionally well, I don't mind telling you. Russell was going individually well and so was I, and so we put it together quite naturally, strangely enough, or fortunately enough.

He was a very educated man, very beautiful family. I came from a situation where I just had my mother as a supporter. I worked at the fruit market. I was doing work that made a bike rider out of me. I'm built like a brick shithouse. He came from Geelong, very well educated, but he wasn't snobby.

We got on well, we didn't worry about who was who. We were friends and that was it. He was a down-to-earth good bloke, a top bloke.

We never saw the best of him. He was the best bike rider I've ever seen. There was nothing he couldn't do. He was a good sprinter, a good time trailer, he just had a lot of natural ability. We could do with a dozen more like him, because he was magnificent, and not only that, he was a bloody good bloke.

Mocka was one of the greatest guys. He'd never do anything to harm anybody...I can only speak highly of him. An incredible bloke. And a bloody good bike rider. But where I would say shit for sixpence, that would be something out of the ordinary for him. No swearing. But he was great bloke. I can repeat stories from Mocka all my life because I loved him. I'm not a poof, but I loved him. I'm an open sort of guy. Always been like that.

Mockridge clearly valued Cox's friendship. "He has always been a good and loyal friend to me. His personality is very likeable and I can recall many happy days spent in his company in Europe."

126

Aged 77 in 2008, Cox is still dedicated to cycling and fitness. He's at Maroubra beach for an hour every morning and at Tempe velodrome every Monday and Wednesday night to coach young riders. He doesn't ride anymore. He doesn't have anything more to prove.

Chapter 12

September 13, 1958:
A Dark Day for Sport

JIM TAYLOR AVOIDS the corner of Dandenong and Clayton roads. The drama that unfolded there that morning in 1958 is still a difficult subject. Two men were run over by a bus that day, but only one lived to tell the tale.

We had started at 10 o'clock from Kelly's pub in Oakleigh, we hadn't gone far, the corner wasn't controlled by traffic lights or anything in those days, just an open intersection.

A black Vanguard had passed us on the right to pull up to do a right-hand turn south into Clayton Road and we were on the left-hand side of the road. This bus, which had picked up passengers – the Vanguard had given way to it – sort of shot across to beat traffic coming from Dandenong.

We never saw him, he suddenly popped out from in front of the car, in our path. He should have seen us because he was sitting up high. So, suddenly, in front of us appears this bus. I had time to sort of turn my right shoulder and I hit it around the front door. I'd just finished a turn of pace and Russell was coming past me.

Next thing I remember, I'm on the other side of him – I started on his left side and next thing I'm on his right-hand side under the bus with him and how that happened I don't know. The bus started to roll backwards towards his legs, and I went to pull him out but I couldn't because I'd busted my shoulder. Russell was already dead, his head was split open. I just scrambled out. It's a bit hazy from then on, but they covered him up, they threw me into an ambulance and raced me to hospital.

There was a coroner's inquest which found that the death was an accident, which was a bit hard to understand, and then a civil damages case came up several years later, brought by Irene against the bus company and the driver, under the old civil damages system, and we were found to be 70 per cent at fault.

We were branded as more than part contributors, whereas we were just riding our bikes down the bloody road. Some of the witnesses said we were doing 35 mph [56 km/h]. I said we were doing between 23 and 25 mph [37 and 40 km/h]. It was impossible with the road conditions to be going any faster.

They normally had a corner steward on that corner, but that day there wasn't one there, for whatever reason I don't know.

That became a big issue in the court case. Our 70 per cent of negligence came into play. In those days the give-way-to-the-right rule was the only rule at an intersection unless it was controlled by lights or stop signs. An open intersection required that we give way to the right and we didn't give way to the right.

We didn't expect to have to stop. We assumed we would ride straight through the intersection like we usually did. We didn't ease down. We'd ridden through there in training and raced through that same intersection, but we weren't aware there was not a corner steward there that day.

We expected to go straight through. We expected there would be a steward there.

Approaching the 50th anniversary of Mockridge's death, Taylor said he had no doubt the collision could have been avoided.

> "We were competing in a professional bike race. A flagman should have been there to guide us through. A flagman could not have stopped the traffic, but he could have indicated to vehicles that the cyclists were approaching, hold up a flag and guide us through."

Two months after Mockridge's death the inquest opened at the Melbourne Coroners' Court before magistrate James Michael Duggan.

First up was Senior Constable Thomas Brain. He had identified the body of Edward Russell Mockridge, aged 30, of 93 Page Street Middle Park, at the City Mortuary on the day he died. He was, Senior Constable Brain told the court, "by occupation a professional cyclist."

Annetta Larsen, housewife, of 352 Princes Highway, Clayton, was waiting for a bus to take her south along Clayton Road to do her Saturday morning shopping. She saw the Ventura bus coming from Clayton slowly cross the Dandenong Road intersection and then saw the cyclists on their collision course.

> I realised they would hit the bus if they kept going. Apparently they did not see the bus because they had their heads down. The bus passed in front of them and the cyclists disappeared from my view. I heard a loud crash and saw a man lying under the bus. The bus didn't stop straight away, but moved on for a couple of seconds and then stopped. Just after it stopped I saw the bus move back. It appeared to roll over the cyclist but I wouldn't be sure.

Thomas William Nicoll, builder, of 15 Prince Street Clayton, also got a view of the collision and the two cars waiting to turn right into Clayton Road.

> They were facing east along the highway and were apparently waiting to allow the bus to pass before making a right-hand turn into Clayton Road. The cyclists came up on the inside of these cars and it is my opinion that these cars obstructed the cyclists and the bus driver's view.

The inquest file shows that magistrate Duggan commented: "It is a very busy intersection. There is no caution light. Before the crash there was no official. There was after the accident."

Leslie James Dunne, traveller, of 12 Belgrave Street Preston, was a friend and cycling contemporary of Mockridge. He was in a car following the scratch bunch. He was not there, he stressed, as an official, but his testimony would be the closest the inquest got to an official or expert view.

> On the 13th day of September, 1958, deceased Edward Russell Mockridge was participating in a road race from Oakleigh to Gippsland. Mockridge was riding with five other cyclists, namely Bill Neil, Peter Panton, George Goodwin, John Young and Jim Taylor, in an easterly direction towards Dandenong. They left the start together at 10.10am.
>
> I was following in a motor car behind the bunch. As I approached the intersection of Clayton Road and Princes Highway, I moved my car to the right-hand lane with the intention of passing the cyclists. Directly in front of me there were four or five cars. When I was 400 to 450 yards [366 to 411 metres] from the intersection, I noticed a passenger bus about to enter the intersection in a northerly direction on Clayton Road.

When I was approximately 40 yards [37 metres] from the intersection, the cars travelling directly in front of me suddenly pulled up and it was then I noticed the bus was still moving very slowly across Princes Highway at what I would say was 3 to 5 mph [5 to 8 km/h].

I stopped my car and saw the bus pass in front of the stationary cars into the path of the cyclists who were travelling in the extreme left traffic lane. The bus was still travelling very slowly and the leading rider swerved and went behind the bus and the next two riders collided with the side of the bus around about the middle.

Mockridge was one of these. He fell to the ground with his head facing the direction to which the bus was travelling and about six feet [1.8 metres] from the rear wheels of the bus. The bus continued on slowly and the rear wheels of the bus passed over his head moving his body. His head then facing in a westerly direction, the bus continued on for about 15 to 20 feet [4.6 to 6 metres]. The driver alighted and ran back to Mockridge and as he did the bus rolled back and came to rest on the legs of Mockridge.

Seeing the collision unfold Dunne ran to Mockridge and attempted to pull him clear of the rear wheels that had come to rest on his legs.

He told the inquest: "The cyclists would not have had a view of the bus until it was almost in their path, owing to the stationary cars on the right."

Questioned by W. McNamara for Robert Alexander Watson, driver of the bus, Dunne expanded on his role in the race.

I was there not as an official, but as an interested spectator. I had two people with me, no officials. The Wholesale Bicycle Retailers sponsor the event and the League of Victorian Wheelmen lay out the rules and precautions. A certain risk of danger is taken by the riders.

Some precautions are taken by the officials to protect the cyclists. They are instructed to keep to the left of the road. If they go to the wrong side of the road they are warned. I am not sure if any other precaution is given for the safety of the riders. This intersection is one of the busiest that the cyclists will cross on this race.

I have seen many intersections policed by our officials. They carry flags. Police have done some work at the request of the League. There were no officials at this intersection on that day. Sometimes there are not officials at the dangerous intersections, but at many there are. This is done to protect the riders.

A speaker system warning cyclists of dangerous spots is another precaution taken by the officials. I don't know where the car was that day. I wasn't at the start when the limit men took off. I saw no sign of the speaker system at the start.

This was as close as the inquest got to examining the conduct of the race and the culpability of the organisers.

It is puzzling that the coroner did not seek to hear from representatives of the League of Victorian Wheelmen or the sponsors of the race.

James Alister Taylor, dairy farmer, of Royal Mail Box 144, Square Forest, Sale, was Mockridge's training partner who injured his shoulder badly in the collision.

This was his formal statement to police:

> The race commenced on the north side of Dandenong Road, at a point about halfway between Warrigal Road and Ferntree Gully Road. We started at approximately 10.10am. We proceeded east along Dandenong Road at a speed of about 22 mph [35 km/h] riding two abreast.

As we approached Clayton Road the deceased and myself were leading the scratch bunch. I was on the inside of the road with the deceased riding alongside me.

When we were about 100 yards [91 metres] from the intersection a car passed us on the off side [right-hand side] travelling in the same direction as us. It slowed down as it approached the intersection and we were catching up with it again. The car entered the intersection and stopped near the centre of the road as though to do a right hand turn into Clayton Road south.

When we were about level with the car I noticed the front of a bus travelling north in Clayton Road come around the front of the stationary car, directly in our path.

I struck the bus with my right shoulder just behind the entrance door of the bus on the near side front. The deceased was riding next to me and would have struck the bus at about the same time.

The next thing I recollect was being under the back of the bus behind the rear wheels with the deceased lying on my left alongside of me. Our heads were facing west.

The bus commenced to roll backwards and I leant over to pull the deceased away but I could not move him and the bus rolled back on his legs. I then scrambled out myself and noticed the deceased had injuries to the head.

Taylor said he looked for traffic at the intersection but didn't see any. "I think the bus was obscured either by the dip in the road or by the car. I thought the road was clear. I had looked and I could see no traffic."

William Robert Neil, a landscape gardener, of 178 Johnston Street Collingwood, was luckier. He was riding at the end of the bunch and saw the bus in time to brake and swerve around the rear of the vehicle.

Constable Denis Francis Elliott from the Clayton police station got a call about an accident on the highway at about 10.15am and was one of the first officials on the scene.

He swore that Dr Ryall of 161 Clayton Road "certified life extinct in my presence." Mockridge was lying on the roadway "on his back, with his head facing northwest."

He estimated "point of impact" as 9 feet (2.7 metres) south of where the body was lying when he arrived.

Constable Elliott and a mechanic from the bus company drove the bus north in Clayton Road to test the vehicle.

The driver applied the footbrake at 15 mph (24 km/h) and the bus came to an "abrupt halt". The handbrake also worked properly according to Constable Elliott's evidence.

The bus driver, Robert Alexander Watson, of 232 Warrigal Road Cheltenham, said that cars obscured his view of the cyclists as he proceeded across the intersection.

> There was nothing to indicate that a bike race was in progress. When the cars pulled up I thought that they were giving me the right of way. To see up lane four [where the cyclists were travelling] I would have to get a little to the south of the leading car in lane three. The cars in lane three did block my view for a considerable distance back to the west.
>
> The cyclists were north of the two stationary lines of traffic. I did see the cyclists as soon as I could physically do so. They did not appear to slow down. They seemed to be going. I got the impression that they had their heads down.
>
> When the bus began to roll back I was between the door and rear wheels. When it started to roll back I got down and started to pull the deceased out. I was in 2nd gear. There are four forward gears. The Transport Board found that the bus was in good condition after the accident.

The Ventura bus company has no record of what became of driver Robert Watson. This is the formal statement he gave to police and which he confirmed at the inquest:

On Saturday morning the 13th day of September 1958, at about 10.15 o'clock I was driving a Reo passenger bus registered number JJ337 north along Clayton Road, Clayton. There were a number of passengers in the bus. As I drove along Clayton Road towards Dandenong Road the road surface was dry and the visibility was good.

A short distance south of Dandenong Road I stopped the bus to allow a passenger to alight. Before starting off again I looked to my right and my left along Dandenong Road. There was no traffic on my right and there was traffic on my left. I waited for a short time until there was a break in the traffic and then proceeded north across Dandenong Road.

Shortly after moving from my stationary position, I saw that the leading cars of the eastern [bound] traffic approaching Clayton Road from my left were coming to a stop. These cars stopped and I continued on at a slow rate of speed.

As I was crossing Dandenong Road I saw a troop of cyclists travelling east along Dandenong Road at what appeared to me to be a very fast rate of speed and passing on the near of the kerb side of the stationary cars. They were riding with their heads down.

The cyclists swerved to the left as though they intended to pass in front of my bus but almost immediately afterwards swerved back to the right into my bus. I heard an impact coming from the near side of my bus and I became stationary within a short distance. The brakes, steering and tyres on the bus were in good condition.

Not quite. Applying a gadget called a Tapley Meter to the brake drum of the bus, Constable Charles Edward Blanks of the Oakleigh police gave evidence on how long it took the bus to pull up when the brake was applied.

In the first test, with the bus doing an estimated speed of 20 mph (32 km/h) – it was a guess as the speedo didn't work – the bus took 24 feet (7 metres) to stop, which was rated at 56 per cent efficiency.

In the second test, the bus took 22 feet (6.7 metres) to stop, rated at 60 per cent efficiency.

Under examination, Constable Blanks said high efficiency would be 80 per cent.

Seventy per cent on an ordinary car would be very good efficiency. Sixty per cent would be good. A passenger bus would need 65 per cent efficiency, he said.

Then he tested the handbrake.

On the first application the brake did not hold on the down grade in Atkinson Street outside the police station. At the time the brake was not fully on but had been normally applied. I then pulled the brake to its fullest extent and the vehicle was safely held at a stationary position.

Despite the brakes failing the policeman's own efficiency test and despite the handbrake not working properly on the first test, the vehicle was deemed roadworthy.

The Mockridge family was represented by barrister Adrian Smithers QC, who seemed to be preoccupied with countering a case of carelessness and wrongdoing that McNamara, for the bus company, was building against the cyclists.

Fifty years on, the record of the "inquisition" is remarkable for what the coroner didn't investigate. It reveals a superficial and officious attitude from the police and a line of questioning from the barrister for the Ventura bus company that was designed to paint the cyclists as careless and culpable.

There were witnesses who said the cyclists were travelling at 30 mph (48 km/h) while Jim Taylor and Les Dunne estimated the speed of the scratch bunch at around 20 mph (32 km/h). McNamara inferred that by riding in the "crouch" position the riders could not see what was ahead of them.

Taylor said he looked for traffic at the intersection but couldn't see any.

Dunne told the coroner the intersection was dangerous and Jim Taylor said the bike riders expected a marshall to be on the corner to warn drivers to exercise care.

Remarkably, no representative of the event sponsors, the Wholesale Bicycle Retailers Association, or official from the League of Victorian Wheelmen, the organisers of the race, were called to explain why the cyclists weren't protected at a dangerous corner at the start of a professional bike race.

To this writer, it is odd that the coroner did not seek to question the people who organised the race to get their account of the day.

Mockridge's father believed that there was meant to be a car with a loudspeaker following the bunch, broadcasting a warning to look out for the cyclists, and that that group was in the pub.

The riders told the inquest there was an expectation that the corner would be staffed. Why were the sponsors and organisers not examined by the coroner?

I put this question to Irene Mockridge in 1999. Even with her strong views on the incompetence of cycling officialdom, she did not believe there was any conspiracy or cover up in the conduct of the inquest.

"The inquest was not a conspiracy. It was probably an oversight that the officials were not scrutinised."

There was no questioning media at the time to delve deeper into the collision or the conduct of the inquest. Journalists in the 1950s were reporters, not investigators. The culture of Australian journalism was by and large passive and dipped its lid to authority. There was no great appetite to take on powerful interests be they reigning political parties or for that matter the world of cycling administration.

The League of Victorian Wheelmen was not without influential advisers. In September 1958 the League would have been in damage control, to use a contemporary phrase.

Journalists covering cycling would also have had to weigh up the costs of criticising cycling officials and their organisation. Information is the bread and butter of journalism and journalists in the 1950s did not bite the hand that fed them.

Jim Taylor believes Bob Mockridge was misguided in blaming the referee and handicapper for not being present in a car behind the scratch bunch when the collision occurred. The officials were honest and honourable men. They would have been packing up and getting ready to follow the scratch bunch. They were hard-working blokes, dedicated to the sport and the riders. They weren't the types to be looking for a beer at 10am.

> Bob was very bitter about it. He believed it was the fault of the organisers that the bus wasn't stopped. I can understand his bitterness, but to be fair we were only five

minutes into the race. The referee and handicapper would have barely had time to get in their car.

There is also no doubt that the rules of the road, and they were simple at the time, said you gave way to your right and the cyclists were on the left of the bus. That's the cold hard fact of the matter.

Of course if there had been a marshall at the intersection, the bus driver would have been aware that there was a group of cyclists coming.

No one can explain the absence of a marshall. There was a marshall on that corner in previous Gippsland Tours.

The death of Russell Mockridge is a black mark against cycling officialdom. The League of Victorian Wheelmen, the body representing the interests of professional cyclists, got off very lightly.

John Burrowes, who finished Mockridge's book, found words about that day that are elegant in a way official words can never be.

He wrote that he and his wife dined with the Mockridges the weekend before the Tour of Gippsland. Mockridge had returned from racing in Tasmania, the book was nearly finished and the mood in the Italian restaurant in Bourke Street was upbeat.

> The following Saturday, September 13, was a fine spring day and was warmed by a pleasant sun, and saw Russell back in the strenuous role of being a professional cyclist again. The Tour of Gippsland was the race in which, as an amateur, he had made his debut in open company in 1947... the irony of life dictated that it would also be his last.

Note: Jim Taylor insists that he and Mockridge were at the head of the pack when the bus came into view. Les Dunne gave evidence that a rider ahead of Taylor and Mockridge swerved and avoided colliding with the bus. Taylor says this is wrong. Les Dunne died in 2002.

Chapter 13

The Supreme Court File

THE DAMAGES CASE against Robert Watson and Clarinda Transport Pty Ltd began in the Victorian Supreme Court before Justice J. Pape and a jury of six on March 24, 1960.

The driver and the bus company were represented by V.H. Belsen of McNamara and Brenton. Irene Mockridge and her daughter were represented by Adrian Smithers QC, assisted by Leo Lazarus.

There was an opening skirmish on the first day when Justice Pape was asked to rule whether the £8,600 raised by the *Sun* newspaper for the widow and her child "should be taken into account as a credit in assessing damages."

His Honour ruled that it should not. This aspect of the case was reported in the Victorian Law Reports of 1960. Unfortunately, the substantial case was not reported and Supreme Court file number 419 of 1959 holds only the official documentation around the case – statements of claim, the defence, affidavits, interrogatories and the like.

The claim was made under the Wrongs Act 1928. The Mockridge claim spelt out the particulars of the driver's negligence in these terms: failing to keep a proper lookout; failing to slow down the bus; driving the bus with defective brakes; failing to apply or sufficiently apply the brakes on the bus; driving at a speed which was excessive having regard to all the circumstances; failing to keep the bus under proper control; failing to give way or any proper warning of approach; failing to exercise reasonable skill and care in the management of the bus; and crossing and blocking the most northerly traffic lane of the Princes Highway at a time when east-bound traffic was approaching...without ensuring it was safe to do so.

The defence denied all responsibility and said the collision was caused or contributed to by the negligence of Mockridge. The particulars of his negligence were set out as follows: failing to keep a proper lookout; riding at an excessive speed in the circumstances; failing to steer or control the bicycle so as to avoid the collision; failing to give way to the motor bus which entered the intersection first and was on his right; passing stationary traffic on the incorrect side so that his view was obstructed or obscured; entering the intersection at high speed without ascertaining whether it was safe to do so; failing to sound warning of approach; entering the intersection from a position which made it difficult or impossible to see whether it was safe to do so; and entering the intersection from a position from which his approach was hidden by other traffic from the defendant Watson.

Irene's replies to questions asked by the defence showed how Mockridge's fortune's changed after arriving back in Australia in December 1955.

In 1956 Mockridge earned £401 through retainers and prize money. In 1957 he earned £2,604 and, in 1958, £3,312.

In the last two years of his life, Mockridge was making money. The average annual wage in Australia in 1956 was £1,373; in 1957 it stood at £1,395; and in 1958, £1,417.

In 1958 Mockridge was earning more than double the average annual wage. (Average annual wages are from the Commonwealth Year Book of 1958.)

Irene Mockridge estimated her weekly cost of living at £20, or £1,040 a year. She declared the family's net income as £295 in 1956, £1,383 in 1957 and £2,190 in 1958.

The jury found in favour of the Mockridges. It found the defendants negligent and awarded the family £20,170 in damages.

But the relief Irene must have felt at this verdict would have quickly evaporated as the jury announced a major qualifier on its finding. The jury also found Mockridge was negligent to a degree of 70 per cent and that the dependents should be awarded just £6,276, or 30 per cent of the total.

Suddenly, £20,170, or £20 a week for 20 years – financial security for Irene and her daughter – was snatched away.

Justice Pape ordered that Irene Mockridge be awarded £6,051 and that £225 be invested with the Master of the Supreme Court to be paid to Melinda Mockridge on her 21st birthday.

He ordered the bus company pay the family's legal costs.

The bus company appealed on the grounds that the amount was excessive. However, by the end of 1960 the appeal was withdrawn.

Jim Tayor then settled his case, with damages set at £3,333, using the same formula that the jury had established in the Mockridge case.

Taylor had snapped his collarbone and badly injured his shoulder in the collision. He did not work for a year and had three years of medical treatment, including bone grafts.

Eventually, he got back on his bike. Today he is a regular rider with a southern suburbs veterans' group, but he avoids the corner of Dandenong and Clayton roads.

Chapter 14

The Greatest All-Rounder

RUSSELL MOCKRIDGE WILL always claim the title of the greatest all-round cyclist of the post-war era. Regarded as a one-in-a-hundred-years athlete, he was hard to beat on track or road. He had extraordinary physical strength but also a strong individualism that set him apart from other competitors.

He didn't need to collude with other riders to be successful. He could be successful on his own. After an exhausting day's ride through the wintry Tasmanian or Victorian countryside, he could unleash a blistering sprint that would give him first place and fastest time.

In post-war Australia, Russell Mockridge embraced the idea of international success and gave inspiration to a community struggling with the realities of rebuilding lives, families and careers after the maelstrom of World War II.

A self-conscious, short-sighted cyclist was an unlikely type to capture the public imagination. For the most part, cyclists of this era were hail-fellow-well-met types, big noters, big talkers. The conversation in a training pack in Melbourne or Sydney was and still is a boastful commentary on success in one's private and professional life. Professional cyclists, with nicknames such as the Professor, the Parrot and the Oracle, played down their training commitment and embellished their success rate in life and love for the entertainment of the pack and the improvement of the story. Why let the facts get in the way of a good tale?

Into this world, in 1946, rode the unlikely Russell Mockridge. He wrote of his frustration with the expectations that success brought, because it came very quickly after winning that Geelong Cycling Club handicap race on his first outing.

> The trouble was that I was still very uncertain that I wanted to be a great champion...I don't think that I wanted to be a great anything. I hated the responsibility of feeling that I had to win so as not to disappoint people. Jack [Baker] and Stuart [Cunningham] [his first coaches at Geelong] had worked so hard for me, my parents had put up with so much inconvenience to help me, and I was glad for their sake I had succeeded.
>
> Today I still have the same attitude to life. I find it irritating and difficult to be expected continually to perform to a standard set for me by others. Despite the obvious excitement of my relatives, friends and citizens of Geelong that I had been named Australia's number one roadman for the [London 1948] Olympic Games, I was comparatively calm at the prospect of a trip to London. It was part of my makeup at this time that I was almost completely indifferent to the events which affected my life. All I asked was that I be as undisturbed as possible. At the time it must have seemed as if I was perfectly suited to being a hermit. Nothing gave me more satisfaction than being alone, in cycling or everyday life. If my parents found me difficult to understand, others must have thought me peculiar; probably most dismissed me as unsociable. There was no obvious reason why I should have been disinterested in the

patterns of life. But none of us can be certain what makes us act in a certain manner. Maybe it is environment, maybe inherited characteristics.

Mockridge was the outsider by dint of his background and because of his pathological shyness.

While this self-doubt and introspection frustrated and distracted him and those around him, it added another dimension to his character.

And in the predictable worlds of the 1950s and 1960s, where men wore the straightjacket of corporate conformity and a woman's place was in the kitchen, it was refreshing to have a public figure who didn't hide his self-doubt behind bravado, and seemed to be seeking an individual path, a road less travelled.

Mockridge gave up cycling in 1950 after competing in the 1948 London Olympic Games and winning two gold medals at the 1950 Auckland Empire Games, to study at college and then university, with the idea of becoming an Anglican priest.

Irene, interviewed by Max Howell for his 1988 book *Aussie Gold* said much that had been written about the religious side of Mockridge's life was off the mark.

> He had a religious urge when he was 19 and 20, but he was just a growing adolescent with serious concerns about the world. He was shy and introverted. During the rest of 1950, while he did not race, he worked at the Victoria Market and kept in good physical condition. The religious infatuation passed and he stopped thinking of the ministry. Essentially he was not a religious person.

This comment does not cancel out the fact that he was seeking more from life. He studied English literature at university and read Chaucer and Shakespeare in that course. His daughter knows he read the 17th-century metaphysical poet and essayist John Donne.

He and Irene read books and listened to Spike Milligan, Harry Secombe, Peter Sellers and Michael Bentine ham it up on BBC Radio's Goon Show.

Like Percy Cerutty, he and Irene were interested in alternative lifestyles. They talked of moving to the country and becoming self-sufficient. He was into health food and believed in mental as much as physical preparation for racing.

Was he depressed? Possibly. He sounds in a wretched state when he writes of his loneliness and isolation. He kept a diary, which he used to write most of his book in 1958. Diary keepers are often tortured souls.

Jim Taylor, his training and road racing partner in 1957 and 1958 said he knew him as well as anyone else.

> He was a quiet sort of guy, never talked about himself or the race or whatever. Bike riders are notorious liars, they'll say, "I haven't trained for a week", yet someone will say they've seen him down the back of Portsea. They never tell the truth about their training because the handicapper might be listening.
>
> A lot of cyclists, they're like bloody parrots, but we'd go training and it wouldn't be unusual for us to meet, say, "How are you going? Alright?" and then we might talk when we got to Ferntree Gully and then get home and say, "See you later." It wasn't unusual to spend eight hours a day training with him on the bike and 25 or 30 words would be all you got.

We used to train pretty hard...I lived in Coburg, he lived in Middle Park. Our training course would be out to Ferntree Gully, up the Devil's Elbow, over the lookout at the top, the last half-mile would be a real *demarrage* (attack) over the top and then we'd come down to Ferntree Gully again and we'd go back up there six times and then we'd ride home.

He had an amazing ability. After 140 miles [225 kilometres] of slogging your guts out in a road race, he could find the reserves to sprint like a demon. He had a lot of fast twitch muscles. He had a very quick burst of speed because of his sprinting background. I had a very fast recovery rate, which meant I could do a turn of pace, have 200 metres to sit off, recover and go again. And I used to train like hell, 1,000 kilometres a week, and that was the only way I could keep up with him.

All I did was ride my bike and eat and sleep, but he didn't have that sort of dedication really, but he'd line up Saturday and he'd clobber you. I don't recall that I'd got to the stage where I could ride away from him, no matter what sort of conditions. Without that focus, he still could achieve.

He had a strong sense of right and wrong, he would never do the wrong thing to anyone and that made him a bit of an easy mark in the world of cycling.

He was a bit different. A loner, that's the aspect of the sport that suited him. You can be part of a team, part of a group, you can have a lot of mates or you can be out on your own. It doesn't matter. There are no dire consequences to being one or the other. Russell was a bit of a loner, a guy who didn't know how far he wanted to go.

He remains a mystery because I was as close to him as others were in his sporting life. He was a well educated bloke. He knew that he had ability, but I still believe he never knew how good he was.

Lindy Mockridge believes her father was talented, but stumbled into the cycling world not really knowing how good he was.

There's a whole lot of factors. There's the whole thing about just walking in one day and massacring everyone else. Just taking off. There'd be a certain level of resentment you'd think. A bit of awe and fascination with the kind of ability that produced that.

And then there was the fact that all the other blokes in the race were working class. I don't think that he would have made anything of that. Personally, that wouldn't have been an issue for him; I don't think he thought about class at all, that doesn't seem to be the way he related to the world. It wasn't a big issue.

I think he was just a very quiet bloke. He was quite bright and he had a lot of sporting ability. He wasn't an extrovert by any means. My mother said to me that his death was really sad in the sense that he had just started to come out of his shell.

Her view of it was she was the extrovert, trying to draw him out. He was the opposite, but he'd just started to be a bit more relaxed about life generally and more open to that, and he died.

He was an introvert. But that doesn't fully cover the picture. I remember my mother saying when he was on the boat with Percy he took on a dare where they climbed in and out of the port holes on the ship. So he was a risk taker. Capable of doing silly things. He wasn't a total wallflower.

Harry Gordon called Mockridge the "Man on the Outside".

He was a lone wolf, and it showed. Following the 1956 and 1957 *Sun* Tours, it seemed to me that he was a man apart from the rest. A teetotaller and non-smoker, he never joined the parties in which some of his rivals surprisingly indulged along the way – and he often took a good book to read during the overnight stops.

At the rest periods, he could often be found sprawled alone beside his bicycle, meditatively chewing on an apple. He somehow managed to preserve his "China Doll" identity, although he took plenty of spills and was always willing to take his turn at the buffeting, bullocking job of going to the front and making the pace.

Gordon finished his chapter on Mockridge with a short description of the man as "the short-sighted cyclist who hated to be hemmed in. When the accident occurred he was, as usual, the man on the outside of the bunch."

Hubert Opperman wrote a tribute to Mockridge for *My World on Wheels* and described him as "the most versatile cyclist Australia has produced...no other cyclist in my experience has been gifted with such a level of overall cycling talent."

He was also a very decent human being.

Chapter 15

John Tressider

SEVENTEEN-YEAR-OLD John Tressider leaned on the fence of the Bundaberg cycling track watching something quite extraordinary unfold before him. It was 1949 and the national amateur track championships would determine who would be in the Australian team for the Empire Games in Auckland the following year.

What was unusual about the racing on the banked gravel track in Queensland that year was that one man was winning every event. He was Russell Mockridge, the 20-year-old phenomenon from Victoria who had come from nowhere to be the number one amateur rider in Australia. The 1,000-metre sprint, the 1,000-metre time trial, the 4,000-metre pursuit, the one-mile (1.6 kilometre) and the five-mile (8 kilometre) all fell to Mockridge.

The junior track rider from Newcastle had a new hero.

"He seemed to do everything so effortlessly. It was obvious he was a great champion even then," said Tressider, who went on to have a very successful amateur and professional career in Europe in the 1950s and 1960s.

Tressider was the 1951 national amateur sprint champion, but missed out on selection for the 1952 Olympics because of illness.

Mockridge mobbed by fans after winning the 1957 Sun Tour, Melbourne.
Reproduced with permission of the *Herald and Weekly Times* Photographic Collection.

Mockridge (left) and cyclist friends in Monaco, 1955.

Mockridge with Raphael Geminiani, France, 1955. Italian-born Geminiani rode for the French team in the 1955 Tour de France and was placed 6th in the overall classification.

Russell Mockridge starting John Tressider in the 1954 Paris Grand Prix. At right is Italian champion Cesare Pinarello, who Mockridge outpaced in the 1952 Olympic tandem event.

Mockridge and Irene in Nice, France, 1955.

Mockridge with his daughter, Melinda, at home in Page Street, Middle Park, 1956.

Mockridge in a motor-paced event at Parc des Princes velodrome, Paris, where the Tour de France finished between 1903 and 1967.

Photo: *Miroir Sprint*

Mockridge training on the North Essendon board track, 1956.

Senior Constable A. Bruckner with Mockridge's bicycle after the tragic accident on September 13, 1958, at Oakleigh Police Station, Melbourne.

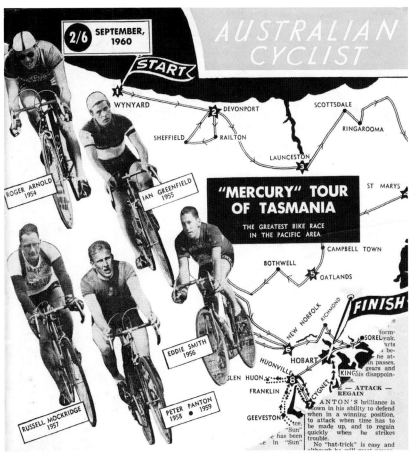

Cover of *Australian Cyclist*, September 1960, showing previous winners of the Tour of Tasmania. Peter Panton, the 1958 and 1959 winner, was in the scratch bunch with Mockridge in the Tour of Gippsland in 1958.

Reproduced with permission of Graham and Josh Huddleston.

The road warrior Tour de France, 1955
Photo: *Presse-Sports*

Mockridge on his way to another victory in the 201-kilometre Victorian championship, 1958.
Reproduced with permission of the *Herald and Weekly Times* Photographic Collection.

He got to know Mockridge between 1953 and 1955 on the European track circuit. Tressider rode in Europe for 11 years.

> What he'd done in 1952 was beyond belief. He won the amateur Paris Grand Prix as an unknown rider from Australia. If you won the amateur you could race with the pros. He shocked everyone by getting into the final against Reg Harris and Jan Derksen, who were the two best pros in the world, and he beat them fair and square. This wasn't supposed to happen. The amateurs weren't supposed to beat the professionals.

He remembers the family's cramped living conditions in Ghent, Belgium.

> The flat was as big as my lounge room. They didn't have heating. They were doing it tough till they went down to the south of France. And I can still see about six clothes lines with nappies and baby clothes. Lindy was in a cot, all in one big room.
>
> The best thing they did was go and live in Nice. He trained in good weather and everything went well.

He also saw a different side of Mockridge: a mischievous, risk-taking young man on and off the track.

"He was a serious sort of guy, but in the right company he was up for anything."

Tressider's Mockridge is a schoolboy prankster who would shimmy up a flagpole to steal an official flag, play a trick on team-mates by short-sheeting their bed or reversing the order of the drawers in their bedroom.

Harmless fun. But stealing a flag from an Olympic compound later cost Dawn Fraser several years of her swimming career. The officials were all-powerful and Mockridge was probably snubbing his nose at their power over the lives of athletes in these antics.

Tressider said Mockridge was shy in groups but good company one-to-one and definitely not a teetotaller.

> He could drink. Even Sid Patterson, who was a big-time drinker, he told me in Paris after they'd raced they went out and he planned to get Mockridge pissed. They were fierce rivals, there was never much camaraderie between them, and he reckons Mockridge out drank him.

> The way I remember him, he was very friendly and witty, but you couldn't get away with generalities. I might say, "gee, it's a pretty quiet day out there despite the heat," and he would say "Really, it's pretty gusty if you have a close look." He wouldn't put you down, but he wouldn't just go along with generalities.

> He was also reluctant to collude and do deals with other riders, and that was resented. That was at the core of the animosity from other riders.

> He was also comfortable living in his own skin. Everyone's different, but he wasn't that different. He was always in a group at the bikes and they'd all be chatting and laughing.

> And as good as he was, he was hopeless as a mechanic. One time in London, he'd come over to ride an amateur/pro event and he didn't have a mechanic, his bike was a bloody disgrace.

> Most of us trackies, we kept our bikes spotless, we'd even clean the sides of the single tyres, put clean tape on the handlebars, but he had raggedy bloody tape on, the chain wasn't adjusted properly, and I thought, "Here's this man, he's a superman, and he had no idea," and yet he was so clever and so good.

He also had great athletic ability as a rower, a runner, and the other story, he had the record in the sand dunes down at Portsea, where he trained with Percy Cerutty.

Tressider said Mockridge's performance in the Tour de France in 1955 was remarkable considering the injuries he took into the race and the fact that he was a sprinter in an international team of road racers who had never even trained together.

He was put in as a helper, a water-boy. There was no way a sprinter was going to win anyway and what he did to ride out the tour was remarkable. He wanted to ride the Tour de France and he did it the hard way.

Tressider renewed his friendship with Irene Mockridge when he returned to Australia in 1960. He believes she was not well supported by the cycling community after her husband's death.

I think a lot of people, once Russell died, just stood there and kept away, and that could hurt too. She battled for years, bringing up Lindy, educating her, doing overseas trips. She was a smart lady in her own right, she did managerial jobs and was well respected anywhere she worked.

John Tressider was 76 in 2008. He lives in Ferntree Gully and still rides a bike for fitness and pleasure.

Chapter 16

John Beasley

JOHN BEASLEY AND Russell Mockridge shared a similar temperament. In Mockridge's book he relates a story about a cyclist who had arranged a 120-mile training ride with Beasley: "When the rider met John in the morning John greeted him: 'G'day' and after the 120 miles were covered, John spoke again: 'Bye.'"

It is the kind of story more often told of Mockridge than Beasley, who turned 78 in 2008.

> He was a quiet sort of bloke, which suited me because I was much the same. Quite often we'd go training and wouldn't exchange that many words. We'd concentrate on what we were doing. He was hard to get to know, but once you got to know him, he was a sincere friend.

Beasley is the first to admit that he was a lightning rod for bad luck when he and Mockridge were together in 1955. A wrong turn in the Tour du Vaucluse in 1955 – one of the major events that Mockridge won in the lead up to the 1955 Tour de France – took him, unnecessarily, over the crest of Mount Ventoux and into snow so deep he thought he was in Switzerland.

Three years earlier he started the 1952 Tour de France with the Luxembourg team after a *Sporting Globe* appeal raised enough money to send four Australian cyclists to France. Beasley was the only one who got a ride, but he crashed on the sixth stage and failed to come in under the time limit.

In 1951 he was the Australian road champion. In 1950 he was the Victorian 150-mile (241-kilometre) champion, an event decided within that year's Melbourne to Warrnambool road race.

The Beasleys are a cycling institution in Footscray. John's father, J. J. Beasley, was a scratch rider in the 1920s and opened a bicycle shop in Buckley Street when John was a toddler. His brothers Vin and Clinton (Clinker) were top-level riders. Vin won the Warrnambool to Melbourne race in 1952 and Clinton gained fastest time in the same race in 1953.

A third-generation John Beasley now runs the family business. The grandson of J. J. Beasley is a successful cyclist and cycling coach.

Mockridge clearly enjoyed having Beasley with him in 1955 as a training partner for their Tour preparation and in the big race.

He wrote of a regular training ride the two would embark on from Nice, into the mountains, and then back to the coast at Cannes: Nice to Puget–Theniers, taking in Col du Vars, then to Annot, then up La Colle St Michel to Thorame, then down to Castellane, a descent to Grasse, then down along the Siagne to Cannes. Then home to Nice along the Cote d'Azur – a total distance of around 200 kilometres.

There's further proof here that Mockridge got great satisfaction out of cycling. The simple pleasures of fresh mountain air, sunshine, dramatic scenery and companionship were pay off for the stresses and strains that went with the job of elite athlete. He wrote:

> These training rides under such ideal conditions did much to compensate me for the less pleasant aspects of cycling. High in the mountains on a gloriously sunny day, I often reflected on my good fortune.

Mockridge's preparation for the 1955 Tour included the 240-kilometre Paris–Roubaix event at Easter, in which he was placed 41st, and the 257-kilometre Tour du Vaucluse in the Avignon region, which he won.

Mockridge was then invited to ride the Rome–Naples–Rome race, where he again met the Italian superstar Fausto Coppi, the 1949 Tour de France winner, who Mockridge, and most of Italy, put on a very high pedestal.

> The enthusiasm of the crowds was the most fervent I had ever seen anywhere, albeit a trifle partisan. Coppi appeared to be about the only one they were interested in and all along the course they chanted his name; high chalk lettering on the roadway, railway embankments and farmhouse walls urged Viva Coppi and dangling banners proclaimed "Coppi, you are our only king."

The next preparation race was the Tour de Dauphine Libere, an eight-day race that decided the final team selection for the French Tour. Mockridge did not finish the race because of other race commitments and Beasley's mixed fortunes continued. He crashed in the area around Briancon and had to wait for a new bike. Then he punctured, but he and Mockridge eventually caught the leaders. Beasley came in 6th among the nine leaders on the stage. By day six, when

Mockridge left the race, Beasley was in 15th place in the general classification.

But on the last day, in heavy rain, he snapped a brake cable on a steep descent and lost 15 minutes while it was repaired. He was not in the finish. But he had earned the respect of his peers for his toughness and was on his way to his second ride in the big lap of France.

Mockridge ran into some bad luck five days out from the beginning of the race when he crashed on his favourite Alpine training ride.

Descending from the 2,250-metre Col d'Allos, he hit water on the road and flew off his bike at high speed, landing badly on the road.

Mockridge's Tour could have been over before it began as he lay in the mist by the side of the road, unable to move his left leg, which was badly gashed under the knee.

A motorist took him to a hospital in Nice, where a gloomy group of friends and supporters gathered that night to reassess their plans.

But Mockridge recovered quickly and, days later, he and Beasley sat down to a celebratory meal in Le Havre. The day before the race, they both woke up with food poisoning.

Beasley rode three stages of the race before a combination of illness, a fall and mechanical trouble forced him to withdraw.

He had contracts for another year in Europe.

I spent the winter of 1955 in England and then came back to start the road season when I had a bad fall in training. I broke my wrist. Luck was against me. I was so despondent I thought, 'It's time to go home.' I got back to Melbourne in August 1956.

Beasley was scheduled to ride the Tour of Gippland in 1958, but had the flu and withdrew.

He is also of the view that Mockridge's death was avoidable.

> There should have been someone there to make sure the traffic didn't go across. The last thing they expected was a bus crossing the highway in front of them.
>
> I was surprised Mrs Mockridge didn't take up a case against the League, because it was definitely the League's fault. They should have stopped all traffic at that intersection, but it just didn't happen.
>
> The riders expected the traffic would be under control. Otherwise they would have been taking more care.

To Beasley, Mockridge was the outstanding all-rounder of his time. He was just as good on the track as he was on the road.

He believes the rivalry with Sid Patterson was more about gamesmanship and publicity.

> It was all hyped up in the paper. Patterson versus Mockridge, and so-and-so wants to meet so-and-so in a match race because he chopped him off last time they raced and he wants to get even. That sort of thing. They used to play it up and it used to get the public in. Down at the North Essendon track they'd be packed out. It was a great crowd puller.

The real rivalry in the 1950s was not between Mockridge and Patterson but between Mockridge and Max and Keith Rowley, the farming brothers from Maffra who had dominated road and track competition since 1946.

Mockridge had knocked the Rowleys off their perch. They were pragmatists and expected the scratch groups to cooperate. Mockridge and other former amateurs, such as Jack Hoobin, didn't always play the game.

> There was genuine rivalry between Mockridge and the Rowleys. They were on top when Mockridge came along, and of course he stole their thunder. He was a much better bike rider than either Keith or Max and they didn't like it.

This is born out in Max Rowley's book, where there is just one mention of Mockridge over 192 pages. Faint praise indeed.

"Names such as Russell Mockride and Barry Waddell come to mind as two more recent greats," he wrote in 1986.

"As well as being top track sprinters, they both had outstanding road performances. It is quite obvious that when they were at their best, there were no other road cyclists about who could exploit any weakness they might have had."

Rowley argues that it is impossible to state that an athlete in a particular sport is the greatest ever, because "there are so many factors affecting the performance of any sportsman or woman that I believe every person who reaches the top is really only the best of his or her own time."

What he is really saying is that he and his brother deserve more recognition in the dangerous debate about "greatest ever" sports stars because their contribution has been overlooked.

Mockridge overtook the Rowleys. He also brought a more stylish presence to the winner's podium. Mockridge was a fastidious dresser. Keith Rowley accepted the inaugural 1952 *Sun* Tour trophy in a tartan wool dressing gown.

Beasley says Mockridge was not a wowser or a snob as he is sometimes depicted. He was before his time in training and race preparation. Some mistook his introspection for aloofness. Before a race he kept to himself, planning the ride in his head. While his fellow riders nervously laughed and joked, Mockridge wanted to be alone so he could psychologically prepare himself for the race.

> He was careful about what he ate, no fatty foods. He always looked after himself well. It's a shame more people didn't get to know him better because he was really a great fella. There'll only be one Russell Mockridge, in my eyes.

Chapter 17

The Inheritance

LINDY MOCKRIDGE HAS accepted the inheritance of her father's talent and celebrity. She's also inherited his looks, his legs and, to an extent, his shyness.

She's also inherited several old suitcases of photographs, newspaper clippings and memorabilia that her mother couldn't chuck out, but couldn't embrace either, because every word and photograph spoke of what had been lost and stolen.

Irene loved Russell Mockridge, but she didn't love cycling.

> Certainly my mother blamed the organisers for it. That the road should have been cleared...she was very angry with the cycling world in the sense that she didn't think she was helped or supported after his death. Whether that's right or wrong, it's true that she got pretty much dropped and people like Bill Long [promoter and official]...I think my mum thought that he might have helped out, given that he had made so much money from my father essentially, but he didn't.

> The race officials should have made sure the road was secure before they used it. But apparently at the inquest the bike riders were blamed, for not looking right.

> I've never heard of a race where you have to give way to oncoming traffic. That wouldn't be a race, it would be a jaunt.

Irene Pritchard was a working-class girl from Richmond. She had to leave school when she was 14, even though she didn't want to. But her mother insisted that she get a job.

> All the teachers begged her mother to let her stay at school, she obviously had talent. But that was outside my grandmother's level of operating. Irene did secretarial work. She was intellectually able. She wanted to travel.

The pair met on the boat to England in 1952. She came back to Australia, where they were reunited in Australia after the Helsinki Games, and married back in London in 1953. Both grandmothers went to England for the wedding.

For three years after Mockridge's death, Irene worked as a personal assistant and administrator in the fledgling Paton advertising agency of Phillip Adams and Fred Schepisi. This opened up a new world and new possibilities.

When Lindy was about seven, Irene went back to the UK for more travel. Irene wanted to train as a teacher, but she was excluded because of an age limit. Mother and daughter lived in the UK and travelled around Europe for three years.

> She did some teaching nevertheless. When we came back she wanted to train as a teacher in Victoria, but again there were some limits to age.
>
> When I was 22 or 23 she did another trip to Europe. It was her chance to do other things now that I was grown up. It didn't really work out. She had ideas of living there permanently, but she couldn't get patriality. So that all fell in a heap, which was one of the reasons she came back. She found it hard to get work, so she came back to Australia.
>
> This was 1979, and in 1980, when she was about 52, she was diagnosed with breast cancer. She had a breast

removed. Almost immediately after that she decided she was going to do a degree so she went to La Trobe University and did an arts degree majoring in history, Pacific studies and English. Consequent to that she decided to do Australian Volunteers Abroad and she went for two years to the Solomon Islands. She was media adviser to the National Council of Women of the Solomon Islands.

Lindy told the *Geelong Advertiser* in January 2008 that one of her lasting impressions from hearing stories about her father was that he liked spending time alone.

The impression of being really shy and a loner were reinforced by the fact that he used to love going on his training rides by himself, or with one particular friend, Wally Smith, and the two of them would go off for hours at a time and not exchange a word.

They would just be in companionable silence, riding along together. He wasn't a great talker in that sense. He used to enjoy his quiet times.

On her mother, Lindy told the *Advertiser:*

He died when I was nearly four but we went to England when I was seven with a cousin of mine who was 18 at the time. The three of us travelled around in a Kombi van for quite a few months around Europe before we settled in England, and I suppose that's a fairly positive, proactive thing to do. It's not just sitting around moping, so I suppose she got over it in a lot of ways, but she never remarried.

You just deal with it, don't you? I think she was very depressed for a while there afterwards. She certainly got some counselling, but not a whole lot. It wasn't ongoing, from what I understand. I think back then there wasn't such a thing as post-traumatic stress, people hadn't identified it. You just basically got on with life and I think that's what she did, whether that was a good or bad thing, that's just the way people operated.

She was determined to be her own person, not just Russell Mockridge's widow. She kept a few friends from that time, but not many. She kept in touch with Johnny Tressider, who was in Belgium with them, and Gino Bambagiotti, Mockridge's manager in Europe, who had connections with Australian promoters and brought the Italian stars out for the Melbourne summers on the North Essendon and Olympic Park board tracks. Jim Taylor, who became the Liberal MP for South Gippsland in the 1970s, also kept in touch.

But she says it is not true that her mother completely cut herself off from the cycling community after Russell's death.

I remember when I was about 16, I presented the trophy to the winner of the Melbourne to Warrnambool race. Mother and I drove to Warrnambool and we were driven around the sports ground in an open-top car. I was slightly embarrassed about the whole thing, but it was a tribute to Russell and mother was a big part of it.

Another reason for Lindy's 16-year-old awkwardness was a matter of fashion. By 1970, the push bike was rusting in the shed, a steel-maker's dinosaur in the age of fossil fuels.

Irene talked to Lindy of lean but happy times in Europe.

She hated Belgium with a vengeance. That's where I was born. Partly because it was the middle of winter and she was heavily pregnant in a cold country with unpleasant people. The people in the apartment they were staying in were not friendly to her. She was very pleased to leave Ghent and go down to Nice. That was a happy period. Except he was going off to race all the time. She had her mother and a baby with her at a flat in Nice. She missed him terribly. She felt quite lonely given it was her first baby and early in their marriage.

Russell sounded interested in everything about Europe. They were pretty urbane, but very poor. That really ground them down. Mother said she had so little money that she became a good cook simply because she had so few ingredients and she had to produce something nice out of very little. So she didn't like the fact that they were struggling and they did struggle. He got ill too, glandular fever, and he couldn't race for quite a while, that was a real problem.

My general impression is that they didn't make a whole lot of money out of it. That was the reason they came back; it wasn't working out for them financially over there.

But there were happy times. Experiencing England and Europe was a coming-of-age journey that appealed to many young Australians who wanted to broaden their horizons and taste life outside parochial Australia.

Lindy said her mother had left-wing views, and she imagined her father would have shared similar views.

The Mockridge family is very straight down the line Liberal. But I can't imagine he would have gone down that line. He was courted at one stage by the Liberal Party to be a candidate, but he didn't want to. My grandfather belonged to the Masons and he didn't want to join the Masons either, so he wasn't into any of that stuff. Certainly she and he used to think about alternative lifestyles even back then.

They had an idea about getting a block of land and being self-sufficient. I don't think he was actively political, more alternative thinking. He was outside the box.

Lindy only knows her father through stories and photographs. An image that sticks in her mind can be found in his book. It is a picture taken during the 1955 Tour de France. Mockridge looks exhausted. He is wearing a racing tyre around his kneck and his face, his glasses, and his Vampire Cycles jersey is covered in mud.

"I look at that picture in the book, with that drawn look on his face, and I think, 'Bloody hell, why did you put yourself through that.'"

Mockridge might have answered her question this way:

Sometimes when I set off on a training ride I think of others who are shut up in stuffy offices or noisy factories, and I am grateful that I can spend so much time in the open air. People often say to me, 'You don't seem like a bike rider; what is there about it that you like?' Well there are plenty of times when I hated the actual competition. But my attitude to the whole business can be summed up if I say: I don't particularly care for being a competitive cyclist but I LIKE THE LIFE. I like the freedom that it gives me. The freedom to spend at least a little time enjoying the things that so many people can only enjoy in the few hours they have outside their working day. I cannot think of anything else that I could do that would allow me to enjoy such a free life. To the conventional this attitude may seem irresponsible. However my life as a cyclist has contained plenty of self-denial and self-discipline. But I look upon the time that I can spend enjoying the freedom from routine as more than adequate compensation for the hard training, sacrifices and sometimes unpleasant and monotonous racing, If there was any other job or profession that I could follow which would allow me to spend as much time doing the things that make me happy, then I could gladly retire from cycling.

Chapter 18

The Finish

When a man dies,
Those who survive him ask
What property he has left behind.
The angel who bends over
The dying man asks what good deed
He has sent before him.

The Qur'an

CONTEMPORARIES HAVE MEMORIES, distorted by time, of the day Mockridge died. Many young riders have heard of him, but there's confusion about his significance, where he died and the circumstances.

As the 50th anniversary of his death approached, I made the time to write this long-discussed book.

On a journey like this you ask yourself "why" many times. It is time consuming, frustrating, it affects family life; your free time is taken up by reading, research, investigation and speculation. There is no pot of gold at the end of it. It is a solo ride and there are no guarantees that your work will be valued by anyone else, never mind a publisher.

Irene Mockridge wanted her husband's memories preserved in a time capsule. Lindy Mockridge has inherited suitcases full of letters and photographs that she doesn't quite know what do with. When Russell died, Irene had to get a job and bring up a child. She didn't have time to be the record keeper and custodian of Mockridge memorabilia. She'd helped get his book published in 1960. She felt her task was done. And she felt the cycling community had dropped her. She didn't feel she owed anyone anything anymore.

Lindy has her mother's stories, but no personal memories of her father. Where was my material going to come from?

In the end it comes down to self-belief. You just have to back your own judgement and get yourself down to the startline.

And there's the bike that once belonged to Russell Mockridge, a touchstone that could bring his story back to life.

My story of the loss of an artefact was thrown into perspective when Lindy told me that several of her father's bikes were stolen from their garage in East Malvern. She, too, went through a stage of anger and grief about the loss of important keepsakes.

Was the Mockridge bike stolen? Was it really Russell Mockridge's bike? There's a cautionary tale here about putting too much store in possessions.

Mockridge himself had little regard for cups and trophies.

The Paris Grand Prix cup, probably his most significant victory outside the Olympics, was given to a mate from Geelong who was staying in his hotel in Paris that day in 1952. According to Geelong legend, Mockridge gave the cup away because his friend wanted it more than he did.

He was seeking truth rather than glory. He gave his possessions away like an early Christian monk seeking to lead a virtuous life. "Blessed are the poor, for theirs is the Kingdom of Heaven." The First Beatitude might have been his motto.

Mockridge and Hubert Opperman made a promotional ride to Albury in 1949, and my father Jack and hundreds of others went down to the Albury football ground after work to see him race around the gravel track. He was a celebrity. He was successful as an athlete but he had other qualities – sportsmanship, generosity, interest in his fellow man and interest in spirituality – that put him in another league.

My mother later said that Eddie Batrouney, a second-hand dealer in Albury, would have "told your father anything to sell him that bike." There was no certificate of authenticity.

The provenance was doubtful, but it was a talisman, real or imagined, that had helped imagine and colour the life of an Australian whose story was fading.

Mockridge was trying to make sense of his talent and the world around him and how the two could be put together for positive results. Those who grew up with his story were impressed by his humility and interest in community service.

He was also seeking enlightenment and fulfilment. He was finding his way on this journey when his body met the bitumen of Dandenong Road, Clayton.

Belief is what matters. Belief in himself gave Russell Mockridge the strength he needed to ride the Tour de France and it let him stand up for values that others only paid lip service to. Self-belief is what allowed him and Lionel Cox, who had never ridden a tandem bike before, to team up and win a gold medal. Unfortunately, belief that there would be officials guarding the corner of Dandenong and Clayton roads on that morning in September 1958 led Russell Mockridge to his death. And there the lesson ended; and began again.

Chapter 19

The Verdict

THOSE WHO RACED against Russell Mockridge knew how good he was – they were almost invariably beaten.

At the time of his death he was the Australian professional road champion and the Australian professional sprint champion – a rare combination in a sport that demands different abilities in the two codes.

He'd been the Australian professional road champion three years in a row – 1956, 1957 and 1958.

In 1956, he set a record in the Warrnambool to Melbourne classic that stood for 24 years.

His time over the 262 kilometres was 5 hours 47 minutes and 5 seconds. His average speed was 44.2 km/h, which made him the fastest road cyclist in the world.

In 1957 he won every major race on the road calendar: the Tour of Tasmania, the Hamilton 75-miler (120 kilometres), the Midlands Tour, the Tour of Gippsland, and the 1,609-kilometre *Sun* Tour of Victoria. He set the fastest time again in the Warrnambool to Melbourne event.

In July 1958, he won his third consecutive Australian road championship and in August won most of the prize money in the Tour of Tasmania.

Russell Mockridge had started life as a road cyclist in Geelong, switched to the track and created a storm in Paris, the epicentre of cycling, by beating the reigning world professional champion in the Paris Open, riding as an amateur. He then won two Olympic gold medals at the Helsinki Games.

He had a rough patch in Belgium in 1953 and 1954 due to glandular fever and the fact that his success had made him a marked man. He was frequently the victim of Europe-based groups that colluded to keep him out of contention.

In 1955, he switched his European base to Nice and started winning. He teamed up with Sid Patterson and Roger Arnold for victory in the 1955 Paris Six-Day race, an extraordinary achievement for three rookies from Australia. He finished a respectable 41st in the Paris–Roubaix race; won the Tour du Vaucluse; and then, injured and ill, rode the 1955 Tour de France, helping the Luxembourg team's star rider to 3rd overall place in the Tour.

According to Hubert Opperman he was the most versatile cyclist Australia had produced.

Percy Cerutty called him the most extraordinary and the most unusual athlete he had ever met.

Harry Gordon called him the best-dressed cyclist he'd ever seen. Gordon also acknowledged his toughness in "the harsh, punishing, rather boisterous trade of professional road cycling."

In 2007 Gordon, the official Australian Olympic Committee historian, placed Mockridge among the 50 greatest Australian Olympians, in the class of Frank Beaurepaire, Boy Charlton, Dawn Fraser, Shane Gould, John Konrads, Kieren Perkins, Grant Hackett, Murray Rose, Ian Thorpe, Lorraine Crap, Raelene Boyle, Betty Cuthbert, Shirley Strickland, Herb

Elliott, Edwin Flack, Cathy Freeman, Debbie Flintoff-King, Marjorie Jackson, Snowy Baker, Ryan Bayley, Kathy Watt and Andrew Hoy.

The French newspaper *l'Equipe* wrote of his 1955 Tour ride: "We take our hats off to Russell Mockridge of Australia. He has earned the admiration of the whole cycling world."

A story that says a lot about Mockridge's sportsmanship and value set is from the 1957–58 Melbourne track season, when he was racing against his old rival, Enzo Sacchi. In a tight sprint finish at the Olympic velodrome the judges gave the race to the local boy, but Mockridge was adamant that Sacchi had won by the thinnest of margins and protested to the judges, urging them to reverse their decision.

The judges declined, but Sacchi left the country with the comment that Mockridge was the finest sportsman he had raced against anywhere in the world.

Trevor Wykes, a Canberra-based cycling writer, said in a 1999 tribute that, "sadly, the 40th anniversary of Mockridge's death passed without remembrance of this outstanding athlete and moral man. Instead, international cycling was plagued by drug scandals and elements of Australian cycling infected with personality politics."

Wykes called on a *Time* magazine tribute to the American baseball hero Joe DiMaggio to express his feelings about Mockridge and his place in the cycling spectrum.

> One sign of a hero is if you feel enhanced simply when talking about him, recounting his feats, recalling a time when your own little life was touched by his.

Mockridge remains an elusive character. His writing speaks of self-doubt and human frailty. His introspection and self-consciousness make his writing formal and dispassionate. He does not give much away.

Like Percy Cerutty, his mentor, he was ahead of his time on training, diet and mental preparation. He had an interest in the spiritual side of life, which at one stage led him to pursue a ministry in the Anglican Church. He was a successful young Australian abroad at a time when Australia had the shutters closed to the rest of the world. He enjoyed "the Continent" and the way Europeans celebrated the sport of cycling.

He was deeply in love with his wife, Irene, who helped point him towards the consistent successes that came in the last three years of his life.

He valued truth, honesty and integrity. He sat lightly on his Melbourne-made bike, his powerful legs driving him to what seemed to be effortless victories.

Chapter 20

Cadence

CADENCE IS THE term used to describe the revolution of the pedals, the number of revolutions of the crank set per minute. It also relates to the rhythm of a spoken piece of poetry or verse, and the fall in inflection of a speaker's voice, such as at the end of a sentence.

In the tight-knit communities of 19th-century Victoria and New South Wales, the poet A. B. "Banjo" Patterson was something of a celebrity. So the engagement of Patterson to Sarah Riley, the daughter of James Riley and Sophia Smith, was big news in the Geelong district where the family was prosperous and well regarded.

But it was not to be. Sarah took Patterson to Dagworth Station at Winton in Queensland in 1895 to visit a school friend, Christina Macpherson and there the eight-year engagement ended in tears. Patterson was smitten by Macpherson and Riley, embarrassed by the pair's behavior, broke off the engagement. Somehow, amid this parlour room drama, Patterson found time to write "Waltzing Matilda".

Sarah Riley was Russell Mockridge's great aunt and this story is treasured in the family. Whether Russell Mockridge valued the poem "Mulga Bill's Bicycle" by his great aunt's former suitor we will never know, but there's a good chance that the mental picture of the bombastic, know-it-all cyclist tearing down a hill on an out-of-control bicycle would have appealed to his offbeat sense of humour. It deserves to endure, like the story of Russell Mockridge.

'Twas Mulga Bill from Eaglehawk that caught the cycling craze;
He turned away the good old horse that served him many days;
He dressed himself in cycling clothes, resplendent to be seen;
He hurried off to town and bought a shining new machine;
And as he wheeled it through the door, with air of lordly pride,
The grinning shop assistant said "Excuse me can you ride?"
"See here young man," said Mulga Bill, "from Walgett to the sea,
From Conroy's Gap to Castlereagh, there's none can ride like me.
I'm good all round at everything, as everybody knows,
Although I'm not the one to talk – I hate a man that blows.
But riding is my special gift, my chiefest, sole delight;
Just ask a wild duck can it swim, a wild cat can it fight.
There's nothing clothed in hair or hide, or built of flesh or steel,
There's nothing walks or jumps, or runs, on axle, hoof or wheel,
But what I'll sit, while hide will hold and girths and straps are tight;
I'll ride this here two-wheeled concern right straight away at sight."
'Twas Mulga Bill, from Eaglehawk, that sought his own abode,
That perched over the Dead Man's Creek, beside the mountain road.
He turned the cycle down the hill and mounted for the fray,
But ere he'd gone a dozen yards it bolted clean away.
It left the track, and through the trees, just like a silver streak,
It whistled down the awful slope towards the Dead Man's Creek.
It shaved a stump by half an inch, it dodged a big white-box;
The very wallaroos in fright went scrambling up the rocks,
The wombats hiding in their caves dug deeper underground,

But Mulga Bill, as white as chalk, sat tight to every bound.
It struck a stone and gave a spring that cleared a fallen tree,
It raced beside a precipice as close as close could be;
And then, as Mulga Bill let out one despairing shriek,
It made a leap of twenty feet into the Dead Man's Creek.
'Twas Mulga Bill, from Eaglehawk, that slowly swam ashore;
He said, "I've had some narrer shaves and lively rides before;
I've rode a wild bull round a yard to win a five-pound bet,
But this was sure the derndest ride that I've encountered yet.
I'll give that two-wheeled outlaw best; it's shaken all my nerve
To feel it whistle through the air and plunge and buck and swerve.
It's safe at rest in Dead Man's Creek – we'll leave it lying still;
A horse's back is good enough henceforth for Mulga Bill."

"Mulga Bill's Bicycle"
 A.B. "Banjo" Patterson

Chapter 20

Career Timeline

Born: Russell Edwardockridge, Melbourne, Victoria, July 18, 1928
Education: Geelong College, University of Melbourne
Married: Irene Pritchard, September 26, 1953, Sydenham, South London
Children: Melinda Mockridge, born Ghent, Belgium, December 12, 1954
Died: September 13, 1958, Clayton, Melbourne

1945   Finishes Leaving Certificate and starts work as cadet
        journalist with *Geelong Advertiser*.

1946   June 22: Aged 17, Mockridge wins the first club event
        he enters. He beats race officials back to the start.

        At second start with Geelong Cycling Club he gets
        fastest time award. After two more wins he is put on
        scratch – the honour mark.

        Jack Baker and Stuart Cunningham, Geelong cycling
        royalty, start positioning Mockridge for the 1948
        London Olympics.

1947   July 26: Aged 19, enters 160-kilometre Tour of
        Gippsland and punctures twice. Takes wrong turn at
        finish and earns nickname "Wrong-way Mockridge".

        Placed 7th in *Sun* Classic 125-miler (201 kilometres).

        Placed third in Victorian team selection trials
        for Australian championship in 125-mile (201
        kilometres) race to Castlemaine and back.

        Wins 125-mile (201 kilometre) Australian amateur
        road championship at Centennial Park circuit,
        Sydney, making Mockridge a certainty for 1948
        Olympic team.

        Wins Victorian 1,000-metre time trial title in 1:15:4.

1948   Embarks on promotional ride from Melbourne to
        Sydney with Hubert Opperman, which Mockridge
        later calls the highlight of his early cycling career.

        Finishes 26th in London Olympics road race after
        puncturing twice.

        30th placing in World Amateur Road Championships,
        Holland.

1949   Leaves journalism and starts work with A. J. Healing
        cycle firm.

        Wins five titles at Australian amateur track
        championships in Bundaberg, Queensland – 1,000-
        metre sprint, 1,000-metre time trial, 4,000-metre
        pursuit, one mile (1.6 kilometre) and five mile
        (eight kilometre), and gains number one spot in the
        Australian team for Empire Games, Auckland.

1950   Wins 1,000-metre time trial and beats 1948 Olympic
        record at Empire Games, Auckland. Beats Sid
        Patterson in 1,000-metre sprint. Overall tally, two
        gold and one silver medal.

        Announces retirement from cycling to study
        for Anglican priesthood. Obtains matriculation
        certificate at Taylors College then starts arts degree at
        University of Melbourne.

1951   Enticed back to cycling. Finishes second to Enzo
        Sacchi at world amateur sprint championships,
        Milan, Italy. A week later reverses the finishing order.

1952   Wins five titles at Australian championships, Adelaide
        – 1,000-metre sprint, 1,000-metre time trial, one mile
        (1.6 kilometre), five mile (eight kilometre) and tandem.

Announces plans to turn professional and refuses to sign £750 Olympic bond.

Meets Irene Pritchard on voyage to London on *Otranto*

July 6: Wins amateur Grand Prix de Paris.

July 7: Wins Open Grand Prix de Paris, first rider to win both amateur and professional events.

Signs one-year Olympic bond four days before cycling events start at Helsinki Games, after intense lobbying in Australia.

July 31: Sets Olympic record in 1,000-metre time trial. In the afternoon, wins tandem sprint final with Lionel Cox. Cox comes 2nd in his 1,000-metre sprint event. Mockridge becomes Australia's first dual gold medal cyclist.

Returns to Australia. Meets Percy Cerutty on ship home.

1953:   June: Back in Europe, wins amateur Grand Prix de Paris second year in succession.

July: Turns professional after one-year Olympic bond expires. 3rd in Open Grand Prix de Paris.

Unplaced in World Professional Championships, Zurich.

September 26: Marries Irene Pritchard at Sydenham, South London.

December: Couple move to Ghent, Belgium, to be closer to European cycling contacts. Little success in road or track racing.

1954   Unplaced in World Professional Championship. Diagnosed with glandular fever.

December 12: Melinda Claire Mockridge born in Ghent, Belgium.

1955   Teams up with Gino Bambagiotti. Moves to Nice,
        France, to start training for summer road season.

        February: Teams up with Roger Arnold and Sid
        Patterson to win Paris Six-Day Race.

        Wins first big road race in Europe, the 257-kilometre
        Tour du Vaucluse.

        Invited to take part in Rome–Naples–Rome classic.
        Finishes 14th in general classification.

        June: Injured in training on Col d'Allos, near Nice,
        five days before start of Tour de France.

        July: A member of Luxembourg-International team
        in Tour de France. Finishes in 64th place three weeks
        later after 4,495 kilometres.

1956   Wins Australian professional road championship in
        Hobart. Mockridge becomes first rider to win amateur
        and professional road championships at first outing.

        8th in Tour of Tasmania after 13 punctures.

        Fastest time in 262-kilometre Warrnambool to
        Melbourne, 18 minutes faster than previous record.
        Average speed of 44.2 km/h claimed as world's fastest
        road race time.

1957   Controversy around Austral Wheel Race. Mockridge
        and Patterson ride in final, but rivalry means they
        refuse to cooperate. Neither is placed.
        1st place Mercury Tour of Tasmania

        1st and fastest time in Victorian Midlands Tour.

        Wins Australian professional road championship
        over Olympic circuit, Broadmeadows, Melbourne.
        Jim Taylor placed 2nd.

1st and fastest time Tour of Gippsland.

Fastest time in Warrnambool to Melbourne second year in a row, riding with Jim Taylor from scratch.

Wins 1,609-kilometre *Sun* Tour with maximum handicap.

1958   Beats former world champion Enzo Sacchi in Melbourne track season.

Mockridge and Patterson meet again in the Austral. The scratch bunch agrees to cooperate for a "best man wins" sprint. Pile up in final lap checks Mockridge's sprint. He is 3rd, Patterson 4th.

Wins Australian professional sprint championship.

August: Wins Australian professional road championship in Perth for the third year in succession.

August: Second in Tour of Tasmania to Peter Panton.

September 13: Tour of Gippsland. Killed in action.

In 2008 Russell Mockridge's ashes were moved from Springvale to a cemetery in the hilltop town of Emerald, where they were placed in a memorial with the ashes of his wife Irene. The couple lived in nearby Belgrave in the Dandenong Ranges when they returned to Australia from Europe in 1955. Those were happy times. The couple enjoyed the peace and tranquillity of the bush. Russell particularly enjoyed the silence.

GEELONG AMATEUR CYCLING CLUB

This is to certify that *E Mockridge*

gained *first place*

in a *24 Mile Handicap race*

held by the above Club at *Geelong*

on the *22ⁿᵈ* day of *June* 19 *46*

from a handicap of *11 minutes*

A. McPherson ....President

E B Beard ....Secretary

Race card of Russell Mockridge, first major win.
Reproduced with permission of the Mockridge family.

Midland-Bassendean Cycling Club
(Under Patronage L.W.A.W.)

presents

125 Mile Championship Of Australia

SUNDAY, 3rd AUGUST, 1958

Prize Money:
First: £40 Cash, Australian Championship Colours, Pennant,
£15 cash extra if using Reynolds Chain
2nd, £20.   3rd, £15.   4th, £10.   5th, £7.   6th, £5.   7th, £3.

To Start at 10.30 a.m.

Victoria:
1. R. Mockridge *1*
2. J. Taylor
3. G. Goodwin
4. J. Young
5. P. Panton *2*
6. G. Chiesa

New South Wales:
7. W. Biddle
8. M. Ford
9. J. Phillips

Tasmania:
10. L. Cubit

Western Australia:
11. B. Waddell *3*
12. R. Host
13. R. Waddell
14. N. Hill *7*
15. G. Maher
16. D. Bentley
17. J. Vogels
18. C. Malcolm
19. L. Bussell

20. C. Newman *4*
21. N. Perrone *6*
22. L. Laing
23. D. Chellini
24. R. Barron

Reserves:
N. Veale *5*
K. Suckling
K. Lehman
R. Cleary
A. van de Putten
A. Stommels

Program for 1958 Australian professional road championship, Mockridge's last major win.
Reproduced with permission of Graham and Josh Huddleston.

Bibliography

Aussie Aussie Aussie: Oui, Oui, Oui! Australian cyclists in 100 years of the Tour de France. Rupert Guinness. Random House, Sydney, 2003

Aussie Gold: The Story of Australia at the Olympics. Max and Reet Howell. Brooks Waterloo, 1988

Australia and the Olympic Games. Harry Gordon. University of Queensland Press, 1994

My World On Wheels, Russell Mockridge, completed by John Burrowes, Stanley Paul, London, 1960

Russell Mockridge: Triumph and Tragedy. Michael Auciello, *Geelong Advertiser*, January 2008

The Rowleys: Golden Years of Cycling. Max Rowley. Caribou Publications, Melbourne, 1990

The Story of the Tour de France Vol 1 (How a newspaper promotion became the greatest sporting event in the world). Bill McGann and Carol McGann, Dog Ear USA, 2006

Why Die? The Extraordinary Percy Cerutty, 'Maker of Champions'. Graem Sims. Lothian Books, Melbourne, 2003

Young Men in a Hurry: The story of Australia's Fastest Decade. Harry Gordon, Lansdowne Press, Melbourne, 1961

WE KNOW BOOK PRINTING LIKE THE BACK OF OUR HAND

A book about a
legendary Australian
cyclist deserves to be
printed by a legendary
Australian printer.

TROJAN

Australia's Best Book
Printing Alternative

Telephone: (03) 94844819
sales@trojanpressbp.com.au